THE LITTLE WORLD OF MAN

THE
LITTLE WORLD
OF MAN

by

J. B. BAMBOROUGH

Fellow of Wadham College, Oxford

LONGMANS, GREEN AND CO
LONDON · NEW YORK · TORONTO

LONGMANS, GREEN AND CO LTD
6 & 7 CLIFFORD STREET LONDON W I

ALSO AT MELBOURNE AND CAPE TOWN

LONGMANS, GREEN AND CO INC
55 FIFTH AVENUE NEW YORK 3

LONGMANS, GREEN AND CO
215 VICTORIA STREET TORONTO I

ORIENT LONGMANS LTD
BOMBAY CALCUTTA MADRAS

First Published 1952

PRINTED IN GREAT BRITAIN BY
LATIMER, TREND AND CO., LTD., PLYMOUTH

To

L. G. FLUKE

PREFATORY NOTE

THE study of Renaissance psychological theory as an aid to the understanding of Shakespeare may be said to have begun, for English and American readers at least, with Dowden's brief essay in *Essays Modern and Elizabethan* (1910). In recent years a certain amount of attention to it has been paid, especially in America. The fullest treatment is in M. L. Anderson's *Elizabethan Psychology and Shakespeare's Plays* (1927). Miss Anderson's thesis is, however, not available to the general reader in this country, and since it seemed to me to need both correction and amplification in many respects I undertook this new study of the field. I remain much indebted to Miss Anderson's work. Some general aspects of Elizabethan psychology are also considered in L. B. Campbell's *Shakespeare's Tragic Heroes* (1930) and Theodore Spencer's *Shakespeare and the Nature of Man* (1943). My general indebtedness to works such as Professor Hardin Craig's *The Enchanted Glass* (1936) and Professor E. M. W. Tillyard's *The Elizabethan World Picture* (1943), will be apparent.

I must record my thanks for their encouragement and advice to John Holloway, of All Souls College, Oxford, and Dr. B. L. Joseph, of Bristol University.

J. B. B.

Oxford, 1951

CONTENTS

Chapter One

INTRODUCTION

IN creating character a writer must, consciously or unconsciously, draw on two main stocks of material. The first and more important will be the result of his own observation of living human beings. It is axiomatic that unless this observation has been keen, comprehensive, and sympathetic, the writer will never be successful in the convincing portrayal of men and women. The other store of material on which he may call is what may loosely be termed the 'psychology' current at the time he is writing. 'Psychology' must here bear the sense not only of the more academic study of Mind, but of all the ways in which an age is accustomed to thinking of human nature. In every age, for example, men tend to expect the mind to work in certain ways, and to be prepared to accept certain conventional methods of representing its workings. To the Elizabethans a soliloquy by a tragic hero was as satisfactory a representation of the movement of thought as the 'stream of consciousness' in a modern novel is to us. Both techniques are valid in so far as they correspond to the actual processes of different types of mind. There are people whose 'interior monologue' takes almost as finished a shape as one of Hamlet's soliloquies, just as there are others whose thoughts succeed each other in the rambling sequence of Marion Bloom's. The Elizabethan dramatists chose—were forced by the nature of their art to choose—to represent all heightened thinking as occurring in one of the forms which it actually assumes, and their audience agreed to accept this. Another convention of 'popular' psychology is that certain physical, mental, and moral characteristics are inevitably found together. This kind of characterization by type is as familiar to us as it was to the Elizabethans; we have a clear picture of what we mean by 'a Blimp' just as they had of 'a Machiavel' or 'a melancholy man'. It is the inferior writer who draws most largely on this source of second-hand knowledge of human nature, but only a very exceptional writer can hope to escape completely from the conventions of his time in his portrayal of character. To a far greater extent than we perhaps realize, our ideas about the actual living men and women whom we think we know and understand are affected by conventional ideas of human nature which we have absorbed from books. The creative writer's conception of human nature is similarly affected, and he has as well the difficulty of representing his characters in a way acceptable to his audience.

In course of time what is purely conventional in a fictional character loses its meaning, and can only be made significant again by the historical imagination. What is eternal, what corresponds most nearly to the unchanging aspects of human nature, remains fresh and true, and re-creates its original impression in the minds of successive generations of readers or spectators. It is natural for critics to try to interpret this vital part of fictional character in terms of the psychological theories of their own day. Indeed, every reader who forms a mental picture of a character in a book does so in the way in which he is accustomed to view the men and women of his own time. Shakespeare has always been recognized as a master in the creation of character, and this method of interpretation has been applied to his figures ever since his own 'psychology' became outmoded—that is, roughly since the time of Dryden. At the present day it is fashionable to describe his characters in the terminology of psycho-analysis, and this kind of appreciation is not necessarily false or valueless. We must, however, remember that the statement 'Hamlet is suffering from an Oedipus complex' is in fact only an attempt to define in present-day psychological terms the imaginative impression made by this fictional character on the mind of a critic. It is obviously not a true statement about Hamlet (who after all does not exist); still less can it be held to be true about Shakespeare's intentions in creating that character. Shakespeare may have portrayed a man to whom we should now apply such a diagnosis, but the idea of the Oedipus complex can hardly have been present in his mind; nor would he, I think, have welcomed it. The crude mistake would be to think that this type of criticism has the same validity as a clinical diagnosis of a living man, but a more subtle danger lies in forgetting that at different times different characteristics are taken to be associated. Because Hamlet evinces some symptoms of an Oedipus complex it does not follow that he is meant to possess them all, and similarly he possesses characteristics which are not present in our conception of the psychosis at all. Any attempt to press Hamlet completely into this mould can only result in distortion; in fact any attempt to interpret the fictional characters of one age in terms of the psychological theory of another must bring some degree of falsification.

This book is an attempt to set out the psychological theory that was current when Shakespeare wrote. It is not an attempt to re-create or re-interpret Shakespeare's characters, nor is it a study of Shakespeare's methods of characterization. Shakespeare's characters have been used to illustrate the theory, rather than the theory to illuminate the characters, and as far as 'character study' has been attempted at all, it is incidental to the main theme. Shakespeare's plays and poems are the chief point of reference, but since the theory was current in substantially the same form throughout the Middle Ages and until the end of the Renaissance, quotation has been admitted from writers as early as Chaucer and as late as Pope. Reference to works other than works of literature has been largely confined to books available in Shakespeare's lifetime in English—works, that is, which Shakespeare could if he wished have read. The major exception to this rule is *The Anatomy of Melancholy*; Burton's great work is too convenient a summary of psychological theory as it was at the beginning of the seventeenth century to be ignored. Quotation has also been made from works originally written in Shakespeare's lifetime but not translated into English until after his death.

Renaissance psychological theory had its roots in Ancient Greece, and in the 2,000 years since Hippocrates it had absorbed material from many and diverse sources. As it stood when Shakespeare was writing it was a combination of the medieval attempt to synthesize all the surviving authorities into one comprehensive system, and the potentially disruptive Renaissance desire to bring into account new discoveries, including re-discoveries of ancient knowledge. Psychological theory clearly illustrates the difficulties of the eclectic approach of the Middle Ages. There were many places where the authorities were in such direct opposition that reconciliation between them was impossible, and alternative views had to be permitted. In fact it is hardly correct to speak of 'Renaissance psychology' as if it were one fixed body of doctrine; there were really several theories possessing a very large measure of agreement among themselves. Many problems existed of which the solution was recognized to be in doubt; many problems had several possible solutions which each writer would repeat without regarding any one as satisfactory or final. Moreover, by the end of the sixteenth century writers on psychology were finding difficulty in making the theory as it were stretch over the facts. If the Middle Ages were faced with a conflict between theory and fact, they usually preferred to sacrifice the fact; the Renaissance had not only more respect for facts, but more facts to deal with. The discovery of the circulation of the blood dealt the old psychological theory its death-blow; it was a fact which just could not be assimilated into the system. But even before 1617 the strain had begun to be felt in psychology, as it had in all branches of knowledge.

Shakespeare had then at his command, if he chose to use it, a theory of Man and his Mind which had centuries of authority behind it, but was not without alternatives, ambiguities and perplexities. But of course Shakespeare did not in any real sense 'use' current psychological theory in his plays. In so far as it was part of the intellectual climate, and automatically affected his attitude to human nature (and also in so far as he found it developed in his sources), it entered into the creation of his characters, but he was not deliberately making his characters fit in with a theory, as to a certain extent Jonson was, nor was he explicitly making use of a view of man's nature for moral purposes, as Milton was. Even had he been writing to illustrate contemporary doctrine about man's nature he could hardly have introduced all the modifications to be found in the authorities. As it is, Elizabethan psychology is implicit in the plays just as Elizabethan political theory is, but Shakespeare does not adhere rigidly to its teachings. Sometimes his characters and their actions cannot be accounted for at all by the theory; sometimes they behave in a way in which, in theory, they should not behave; sometimes we can find theoretical justification for what they do, but only by the use of such fine-drawn arguments that we may feel sure that Shakespeare would be surprised—if also, we may hope, touched—by our efforts. It is obvious that Shakespeare gave his imaginative grasp of human character precedence over all convention, and rightly so. A knowledge of Renaissance psychology will not explain all of Shakespeare's characters, or all of any one of them. Still less will it explain the process of creation; it is the property of genius to be inexplicable. Nevertheless there are many places where a knowledge of current psychology is a help to the understanding of what Shakespeare intended, and some places where it is essential. It is equally important for the understanding of many—one might say, all—writers from Chaucer to Milton. By studying the theory of Man and his mind in 1600, we may grasp at least part of what went to the making of Shakespeare's characters, and perhaps not least importantly, we shall be prevented from some misconceptions.

II

Elizabethan writers thought it proper to begin their studies of Man by placing him in his position in the Universe, and it is best to follow their example. Their view of Man was dominated by two major concepts, that of the Great Chain of Being, and that of Man as Microcosm. Much has recently been written on the Great Chain, the vast system of gradations which linked everything in the Universe from the merest stone on Earth to the Almighty Himself, in an infinite series of progressive stages. Based on the fundamental principles of the Plenitude of God and the Continuity of His Creation, it permitted no exceptions, no disruptions in its orderly sequence of ascending powers. Perhaps the best-known summary of the system is that of Pope, in the *Essay on Man*:

> See, through this air, this ocean, and this earth,
> All matter quick, and bursting into birth.
> Above, how high, progressive life may go!
> Around, how wide! how deep extend below!
> Vast chain of being! which from God began,
> Natures ethereal, human, angel, man,
> Beast, bird, fish, insect, what no eye can see,
> No glass can reach; from infinite to thee,
> From thee to nothing.—On superior powers
> Were we to press, inferior might on ours;

> Or in the full creation leave a void,
> Where, one step broken, the great scale's destroyed:
> From Nature's chain whatever link you strike,
> Tenth, or tenth thousand, breaks the chain alike.[1]

Only the Devils in Hell had no part in the great Ladder. The principle of gradation was continued within the classes of objects which went to make up the Chain: one example of the species was superior to its fellows, and provided the link with the class above. Beasts recognized their King in the Lion; fish theirs in the Dolphin; even stones had their sovereign.

Man's position in the Great Chain was a vitally important one. He was the natural Lord of all terrestial beings, the next highest creation to the Angels. In one respect he was even superior to the Angels, for he had the power of Learning, which they, being created in possession of all knowledge, could not possess. As the only earthly creature enjoying the power of Reason, Man was the only channel through which the knowledge of God could enter the world. He was perhaps also the only means by which Higher Creation could gain knowledge of sensual life; the Son had to become Man to endure fleshly torment. Sir John Davies summarizes his position thus:

> God first made Angels bodilesse pure minds,
> Then other things which mindlesse bodies bee;
> Last he made man th' *Horizon* twixt both kinds,
> In whom we do the world's abridgement see.[2]

Man was the living link between Mind and Matter; his Soul joined the sublunary and the celestial. This position had its especial responsibilities. Man was given greater powers than plants or beasts for one main purpose: that he might come to the knowledge and love of God:

> Therefore we understand by the reasonable soule and life, such a soule and life as hath counsell, judgement and reason, and which was created to this end, that knowing God her Creator, and loving him in respect thereof, she might honour and serve him, and finally by degrees attaine to immortal life and happinesse, which is appointed for her ende. For as nothing is more excellent then reason, whereof God hath made man partaker, so ther is nothing more beseeming reason then to know, love and honour God, seeing there is nothing

greater, more excelle*n*t, or that may be compared unto him. . . .
Therefore God hath not given such a life to stones as he hath given
to trees and plants, nor yet sence, imagination, and fantasie to trees
and pla*n*ts, as he hath done to beastes; so he hath not graunted reason
to beastes, as hee hath to men, and that not without just cause.[3]

Stones are merely required to be, and are therefore inanimate.
Plants must live and grow, and need a 'Vegetable Soul' to
govern their powers of nutrition and 'augmentation'. Since
beasts possess the power of movement, they must have a 'Sensible' Soul capable of experiencing sensation and emotion, and
some power of thought to direct their motions. Man in addition
must know God, and is therefore given a Rational Soul.

It was part of the doctrine of the Great Chain that each stage
of the ladder ascending up to God possessed the qualities of all
the stages below it. Raphael tells Adam that it is even the case
that angels need food as human beings do.[4] 'Vegetable' and
brutal qualities were therefore included in Man's nature, of
which the distinguishing feature was that it combined the highest
and lowest faculties. In Pope's words again, Man was

> In doubt to deem himself a God, or beast.[5]

Donne, in a verse Letter, develops the thought:

> Man is a lumpe, where all beasts kneaded bee,
>   Wisdome makes him an Arke where all agree;
> The foole, in whom these beasts do live at jarre,
>   Is sport to others, and a Theater;
> Nor scapes hee so, but is himselfe their prey,
>   All which was man in him, is eate away,
> And now his beasts on one another feed,
>   Yet couple'in anger, and new monsters breed.
> How happy 'is hee, which hath due place assign'd
>   To 'his beasts, and disaforested his minde!
> Empail'd himselfe to keepe them out, not in;
>   Can sow, and dares trust corne, where they have bin;
> Can use his horse, goate, wolfe and every beast,
>   And is not Asse himselfe to all the rest.
> Else, man not onely is the heard of swine,
>   But he's those devills too, which did incline
> Them to a headlong rage, and made them worse:
>   For man can adde weight to heavens heaviest curse.[6]

As Donne makes plain, these bestial qualities, although in themselves not necessarily bad, required to be kept in check by the higher powers of the mind. The principle of Order was of course vital to the concept of the Great Chain; each step in the ladder was lord over all the steps below, and in its turn servant of the steps above. Pride, disobedience and rebellion were the capital offences against this law, and their Original was Satan. This was also the law of Human Nature; in man, the 'abridgement' or 'epitome' of the World, the god-like faculty of Reason must exercise the same supreme authority as God in the Universe, or God's representative, the King, in the State.

The Fall, however, had disrupted the Golden Chain, so that lower forms of existence could rebel against, and even temporarily overcome, the higher:

> And where all the meane causes of things even from the uppermost heaven, unto the lowest part of the earth, depended each upon other in such an exact order and uniformity to the production of things in their most perfection and beautie, so as it might well be likened to that *Aurea Cathena* as *Homer* calleth it, by the grievous displeasure, which God conceived against man, he withdrew the vertue which at first he had given to things in these lower parts, and nowe through his curse the face of the earth and all this elementarie worlde, doth so much degenerate from his former estate, that it resembleth a chaine rent / in peeces, whose links are many lost and broken, and the rest so slightly fastened as they will hardly hang together. . . .[7]

The first result of Adam and Eve's transgression is the rebellion of their lower faculties against their reason:

> They sate them down to weep, nor onely Teares
> Raind at thir Eyes, but high Winds worse within
> Began to rise, high Passions, Anger, Hate,
> Mistrust, Suspicion, Discord, and shook sore
> Their inward State of Mind, calme Region once
> And full of Peace, now tost and turbulent:
> For Understanding rul'd not, and the Will
> Heard not her Lore, both in subjection now
> To sensual Appetite, who from beneath
> Usurping over sovran Reason claimd
> Superior sway. . . .[8]

The control of the Reason in Man might be overthrown, and the brutal elements in him allowed to run riot, either temporarily or permanently. Temporary overthrow of the Reason might be caused by illness, by drunkenness, or by passion, particularly by the passion of anger. The different stages of drunkenness were sometimes classified according to the different beasts which they resembled;[9] Milton uses this idea in *Comus*, where the 'pleasing poison' from the 'baneful cup'

> The visage quite transforms of him that drinkes
> And th'inglorious likeness of a beast
> Fixes instead, unmoulding reason's mintage
> Character'd in the face.[10]

Drunkenness, rage and madness were usually (following Aristotle) regarded as akin. Thus Cassio ruefully observes:

> It hath pleas'd the divell drunkenness, to give place to the divell wrath: one unperfectness, shewes me another, to make me frankly despise myself.*

The tag *Ira furor brevis est* was a commonplace: Hall expands the idea, noting that there is

> no difference between anger and madness, but continuance; for, raging anger is a short madness. What else argues the shaking of the hands and lips, paleness, or rednesse, or swelling of the face, glaring of the eyes, stammering of the tongue, stamping with the feet, unsteady motions of the whole body, rash actions we remember not to have done, distracted and wilde speeches? And madnesse again is nothing but a continued rage, yea some madnesse rageth not: such a milde madness is more tolerable, than frequent and furious anger.[11]

Lear's madness, therefore, was a natural development from his choler, a continued instead of an intermittent deprivation of reason. Supersession of the Reason by any violent emotion was a temporary madness, and it was arguable that a man subject to repeated fits of passion could not be judged wholly sane. At all

---

* *Othello*, ii, iii, 302–3. (Except where otherwise stated, quotations of Shakespeare are taken from the First Folio. In these and in other quotations from sixteenth- and seventeenth-century works the use of 'u', 'v', 'i', and 'j' has been modernized. Act, scene, and line references to Shakespeare are from the 'Arden' edition of the plays.)

B

events, a passionate man, unless he exercised a conscious self-control, would find his outbursts becoming more violent and more frequent until, perhaps, he could truly be called mad. It was also true that a man liable to fits of passion over trivial matters might find himself overwhelmed, as Lear is, when a serious cause for passion presented itself.

Genuine madness—that is, the complete and continuous deprivation of reason—could, as Hall says, be of two types. Calm madness, most often given the generic name of 'Melancholy', was the less serious, or at any rate the less disturbing. Its real danger was that it easily assumed the form of the deadly sin of Despair, and resulted in self-murder. The sufferer was on the whole to be treated sympathetically, and efforts had to be made to relieve his gloom. Furious madness, on the other hand, demanded harsher treatment; the lunatic must be restrained, if necessary in chains, lest he do damage to himself and others. Since his wild fancies were the product of an over-active brain, he must be kept from stimulatives; hence starvation and the solitary, darkened cell. It might finally be necessary to bring him to reason by force, and so the whip was employed. It is easy to-day to shudder at the barbarous Renaissance treatment of the insane, and to welcome the more enlightened, 'modern' views of men such as Johann Weyer. It must be remembered that, however wrong they were in their treatment, the Elizabethans at least believed themselves to have scientific reason for what they did, although we may see in their attitude a survival not only of a Dark Age belief in possession but of an even more primitive horror of the exceptional and inexplicable.

Of more direct interest to us is Shakespeare's depiction of his three mad heroes, Othello, Lear and Timon. Timon's madness, of course, is different in kind from that of the other two; it is permanent, and it takes the form of a settled misanthropy instead of violence and fury. The overthrow of the reason in all three is made manifest, as might be expected, in the illogicality of their words and deeds, the violence and changeability of their moods, and the feverish disorder of their imagination. The upsurge of brutishness in them is shown largely by their preoccupation with sexual matters. This might not be remarkable in *Othello*, where the dominant motive is sexual jealousy, but its presence in *Lear* and *Timon* has aroused comment. It has even been suggested that it corresponds to a mood of 'sexual revulsion' in Shakespeare himself, and this is no doubt possible. At the same time it is obviously not easy to represent dramatically a revolt of the lower faculties of Man—that is, Growth, Nutrition and Reproduction. They cannot, in fact, be shown in action, but only as imagery. In *Timon*, use is made of images of unnatural growth,[12] but of the three faculties it is Sex which offers the greatest scope for effective rhetoric. It may be that in his attempts to display the workings of these disordered minds Shakespeare was almost automatically forced into an emphasis on the most obviously bestial, and at the same time, from the poet's point of view, most powerfully emotive aspect of human nature. It is of course indicative of the derangement in the minds of these heroes that they see only the unpleasantness of sex, and regard it as a dominant in the life of Man, instead of as a natural part in the universal scheme. In Lear's ravings, Sex shares its place with a consideration of Superfluity, and in Timon's with Greed. It is apparent that Shakespeare associated Lust with the bestial qualities of Ravin and Gluttony:

> The expence of Spirit in a waste of Shame
> Is Lust in action, and till action, lust
> Is perjurd, murdrous, blouddy full of blame,
> Savage, extreame, crude, cruell, not to trust. . . .[13]

This association would make it easier for Lust to assume the role of a symbol of Bestiality in the overthrow of the mind.

To yield to excess passion was to yield to Sin, and Sin itself was bestial:

> If wee had the witte to conceive the baseness of sinne, or from what abject Parentage it is sprung, we should hate it as a Toade, and fly from it as an Adder. Not without reason have manie learned Wryters called it Bestiall, for it is all derived and borrowed from Beastes. Pride and inflammation of hart we borrow from the Lion, avarice from the Hedghog, luxury, ryot and sensuality from the Hogge: and therefore we call a leatcherous person a boarish companion. Envy from the Dogge, Ire or wrath from the Wolfe, Gluttony or gurmandise from the Beare, and lastly sloth from the Asse. So that as wee apparaile our selves in Beastes skinnes, in self same sort we clothe our soules in theyr sinnes.[14]

The disguised Edgar characterizes himself in bestial terms:

> False of heart, light of eare, bloody of hand; Hog in sloth, Foxe in stealth, Wolfe in greedinesse, Dog in madnes, Lyon in prey.[15]

This type of symbolism goes back to the moralized bestiaries; it recurs when the companies of beasts attack the House of Alma in the second book of the *Faerie Queene*.[16] In *Troilus and Cressida*, Ulysses' great speech on Order ends with a bestial image—the wolf, so often used by Shakespeare as the type of ravin—to express the consequences of a general subversion.[17] Chaucer's Parson clearly puts the relation between Sin and the overthrow of the divine principle of Order:

> And ye shul understonde, that in mannes synne is every manere of ordre or ordinance turned up-so-doun. / For it is sooth, that god, and resoun, and sensualitee, and the body of man been so ordeyned, that everich of thise foure thynges sholde have lordshipe over that other; / as thus: god sholde have lordshipe over reson, and reson over sensualitee, and sensualitee over the body of man. / But soothly, whan man synneth, al this ordre or ordinance is turned up-so-down. / And therfore, thanne, for-as-muche as the reson of manne ne wol nat be subget ne obeisant to god, that is his lord by right, therfore leseth it the lordshipe that it sholde have over sensualitee, and eek over the body of man. / And why? For sensualitee rebelleth thanne agayns resoun, and by that way leseth resoun the lordshipe over sensualitee, and over the body./ For right as resoun is rebel to god, right so is bothe sensualitee rebel to resoun and the body also.[18]

The maintenance of due order and degree in the nature of man was not only essential to physical and mental health; it was in the truest sense a spiritual necessity.

III

The concept of Man as Microcosm was also fundamental to Elizabethan psychology:

> the body of man is no other but a little modell of the sensible world, and his soul an Image of the world intelligible,[19]

states Romei categorically, and the parallels between the little world of Man and the great world of which he was the epitome were carried to remarkable lengths. Helkiah Crooke begins his textbook on human anatomy with a long series of correspondences:

> The ancient Magitians (for so naturall Philosophers were of old tearmed), as also the great wise Priests of the Egyptians, did make of this whole universe, three parts: the one, uppermost or superior, which they tearmed the intellectuall and Angelical part, the seat of the *Intelligentiae* . . . by whose direction and command the inferior or lower world is guided and governed; another middle, which they termed the heavenly part, in the middest whereof, the Sun ruleth, as leader and moderater of the rest of the Stars: the 3. sublunary, or Elementary, which is admirable and abundantly fertile, in procreating, increasing and nourishing of creatures and plants.

These three divisions of the Universe are matched by the three main parts of the human body:

> The head, the Castle and tower of the Soule, the seate of reason, the mansion house of wisdome, the treasury of memory, judgement and discourse, wherein mankind is most like to the Angels or intelligencies, obtaining the loftiest and most eminent place in the body; doth it not elegantly resemble that supreame and Angelicall part of the worlde? The middle and celestiall part, is in the breast or middle venter, most exactly, and even to the life expressed. For as in that celestiall part, the Sun is predominant, by whose motion, beames and light, all things have brightnesse, luster and beauty; so in the middest of the chest, The heart resideth, whose likeness and proportion to the Sun, is such and so great, as the ancient writers have been so bolde as to calle the Sun / the heart of the world, and the heart the Sunne of man's bodie. . . . Now further, who seeth not the sublunary part of the world expressed in the inferior venter or lower belly? for in it are contained the parts that are ordained for nourishment and procreation, so as we neede not make any doubt to professe and affirme, that all things are found in the body of man, which this universall world doth embrace and comprehend.

Crooke goes on to trace in the microcosm correspondences to the planets—to the Moone, the brain; to Jupiter, the liver; to Mars, the gall-bladder; to Saturn, the spleen, and so on. Our eyes when we are angry dart forth flashes like lightning, while

> the rumbling of the guts, their croaking murmurs, their rapping escapes, and the hudled and redoubled belchings of the stomacke, do represent the fashion and manner of all kindes of thunders . . .[20]

All this may seem ludicrous to us, but Crooke was no visionary engaged in finding mystical 'evidences' of the Almighty; he was a typical mind expounding a traditional view. He deemed it right to point out the divinely ordained similarity of man's body to the Universe before he went on to his sober discussion of its anatomy.

The ultimate ground for these elaborate correspondences was that Man, like all created things, was a mixture of the four elements. He was therefore of one nature with everything in the Universe. Added to this was the thought that Man, as the last-created thing, must sum up all the previous handiwork of God. The medieval passion for analogy had done the rest; for that matter the desire to find 'emblems', 'hieroglyphs' or 'signatures' of God in that portion of His Creation in the compass of Man's knowledge was certainly not extinct as late as Sir Thomas Browne. Man as the noblest work of God must *a fortiori* give evidence of the design of His Universe. This type of thinking would naturally tend to break up under the impact of new scientific discovery, and still more of the new scientific attitude of mind; but to a certain extent this tendency was off-set in the earlier seventeenth century by the undercurrent of interest in Hermetic Philosophy, which had a vested interest in the belief in correspondence and 'sympathy' (or interaction) between the different parts of the Universe.

The parallel between the body and the State was almost as important as that between the body and the Universe:

> The commonweale with all her parts, orders, qualities, and requisites whatsoever is (for better apprehension and illustration) set forth by sundry fit resemblances, as by the architecture of an house, by the swarming and cohabiting of Bees in a hive, by a ship floating on the sea and such like; but by none more properly than eyther by the universall masse of the whole world . . . or else by the body of man, being the lesser world, even the diminutive and modell of that wide-extending universall.[21]

The best-known example of this parallel in Shakespeare is Menenius' discourse on the Belly in *Coriolanus*;[22] this speech was of course a commonplace. In his political plays—that is, the Histories, *Macbeth*, *Julius Caesar* and *Coriolanus*—Shakespeare frequently speaks of the body politic in terms of the human body.

He very often, for example, likens civil disturbance to bodily illness. He also, though less frequently, likens the body to a Commonwealth:

> Betweene the acting of a dreadfull thing
> And the first motion, all the *Interim* is
> Like a *Phantasma* or a hideous Dreame:
> The *Genius*, and the mortall Instruments
> Are then in councell; and the state of man,
> Like to a little Kingdome, suffers then
> The nature of an Insurrection.[23]

In *King John* and again in *2 Henry IV* there are striking passages where the body of the King and the body of the State are almost identified. In describing the condition of England after the death of Arthur, John says:

> Nay, in the body of this fleshly Land,
> This kingdome, this Confine of blood, and breathe
> Hostilitie and civill tumult reignes
> Betweene my conscience, and my Cosins death.[24]

After his accession, Henry V promises amendment in his life:

> The Tide of Blood in me,
> Hath prowdly flow'd in Vanity, till now.
> Now doth it turne, and ebbe back to the Sea,
> Where it shall mingle with the state of Floods,
> And flow henceforth in formal Majesty.
> Now call we our High Court of Parliament,
> And let us choose such Limbes of Noble Counsaile,
> That the great Body of our State may go,
> In equall ranke, with the best govern'd Nation.[25]

In this last passage the full range of correspondences is present between the Body, the State and the World.

Direct formal parallelism between the Body and the Universe is generally reserved for the description of superhuman characters. Menaphon speaks of Tamburlaine much as Cleopatra speaks of Antony:

> 'Twixt his manly pitch,
> A pearle, more worth then all the world, is plaste,
> Wherein by curious soveraintie of Arte,
> Are fixt his piercing instruments of sight:
> Whose fiery cyrcles bear encompassed
> A heaven of heavenly bodies in their Speares . . .

His face was as the Heav'n, and therein stucke
A sunne and Moone, which kept their course, and lighted
The little O, th'earth.[26]

In Shakespeare (and his contemporaries) such parallels occur most frequently in tragedy, where they serve to bring out the grandeur of the hero and the importance of his actions. But an Elizabethan sonneteer could not speak of his mistress' eyes as stars, or write of the tempest in his soul and the rain of tears bedewing his cheeks, without referring however conventionally to this view of Man.

The concept of the Great Chain gave to psychology a sense of the necessity of Order; the concept of Man as Microcosm emphasized the importance of Harmony to the soul. The primeval state of matter was the chance conflict of the elements which Milton describes in Book II of *Paradise Lost*.[27] At the creation 'light shone, and order from disorder sprong'.[28] Separated and reduced to order, the elements could be thought of as arranged in gradation according to their density, as they are found in the universe: Earth as the centre; next Water (the sea); then Air; and uppermost Fire—that is, the stars. Each element, however, possessed two of the four 'primary qualities' of Heat, Cold, Dryness and Moisture, and each primary quality was shared by two elements. The elements thus formed as it were a circle with joined hands, continually kept in motion by their mutual attraction and repulsion.[29] Again, a major characteristic of the elements was Mutability; they were continually changing one into another by a process of rarefaction or condensation. (A simple analogy would be the change in the single element water from a solid to a liquid and so to a gas.) This changing could not be directly observed in nature, since it was not possible to isolate (to use modern terminology) these instable substances:

> Such elements are only to be conceived in youre minde, being it is not granted to any external sense to handle them in their pure and absolute nature.[30]

In the world, the elements were only found in impure and mixed forms. The motion of the elements or their 'qualities' could be thought of as a dance, as Sir John Davies describes it:

Daucing, bright lady, then began to be,
    When the first seedes whereof the world did spring,
The Fire, Aire, Earth and water, did agree,
    By Love's persuasion, Nature's mighty King,
To leave their first disordred combating,
    And in a daunce such measure to observe,
    As all the world their motion should preserve.

Since when they still are carried in a round,
    And changing come one in anothers place,
Yet do they neyther mingle nor confound,
    But every one doth keep the bounded space
Wherein the daunce doth bid it turne or trace.
    This wondrous myracle did Love devise,
    For Daucing is Love's proper exercise.[31]

Love, music and dancing were all closely associated in the Elizabethan mind. They were types of the harmonious reconciliation
of opposites and the friendly co-operation of units which at the
same time retained their own identity. The dance of the elements
corresponded to the rhythmical motion of the Heavens, which
was audible to the liberated soul as the music of the Spheres.
Castiglione regards a knowledge of music as necessary to the
noble man because it 'harmonizes' or composes the soul. It was
for this reason that music was played to soothe the disturbed
minds of madmen, as it is to Christopher Sly and to Lear. Elyot
recommends that music should be taught to children

for the better atteynynge the knowledge of a publike weale, which
. . . conteyneth in it a perfect harmony,

and interprets dancing as a symbol of marriage and concord.[32]
The fullest expression in Shakespeare of the correspondent har-
monies of the universe and the soul is in the last act of *The
Merchant of Venice*. Every Elizabethan would agree with Lorenzo's 'sentence':

The man that hath no musicke in himselfe,
Nor is not moved with concord of sweet sounds,
Is fit for treasons, stratagems, and spoyles . . .[33]

Such a man would be, like Jaques, a malcontent, 'compact of
jars'. When music was thus the type of unity in diversity in the

World, the State, the human race, and the individual soul, it is
not surprising to find it used in Shakespeare's last plays to sym-
bolize reconciliation and the restoration of harmonious personal
relationships.

A disturbance of any one part of the Universe would necessarily affect the whole framework of Nature. Hooker makes this
clear when he is discussing natural law:

> For wee see the whole world and each part thereof so compacted that
> as long as each thing performeth onely that worke which is naturall
> unto it, it thereby preserveth both other things and also it selfe. Con-
> trariwise let any principall thing, as the Sunne, the Moone, or any
> one of the heavens or elements, but once cease or faile, or swarve;
> and who doth not easily conceive that the sequele thereof would be
> ruine both to itselfe and whatsoever dependeth on it?

As an integral and important part of the fabric of Nature, Man
could by his conduct affect the workings of the Universe:

> is it possible that man, being not onely the noblest creature in the
> world but even a very world in himselfe, his transgressing the law of
> his nature should draw no manner of harme after it?[34]

Thus it is that Macbeth's crime is followed by unnatural events
both in the Heavens and on earth, and the chaos in Lear's mind
is echoed by the storm. The harmony of Man's soul was an integral part of the harmony of the Universe, just as the order
within him was part of the divine Order. Since after the Fall
that harmony and order within man were easily disturbed, the
movements of man's soul possessed a cosmic significance.

IV

Even in his corrupt state, Man's position in the Universe was
one of great, even if uncertain, glory. But compared to unfallen
Man he was a pitiful creature, subject to countless trials and
miseries. By the Fall our first parents lost their pure unclouded
knowledge of God—'*Battes* they became that *Eagles* were before',
says Sir John Davies[35]—and we remain in bewildered darkness
and ignorance of His purposes. By the Fall Man's body became
subject to illness and death, and his soul to Sin, which is spiritual
illness and death. Everything, including his own nature, con-

spired against Man's sovereignty; his only trust was in the infinite grace and goodness of God. Renaissance writers move easily from a consideration of Man's nobleness to a consideration of his infirmities. Burton begins *The Anatomy of Melancholy* with a resounding list of Man's titles:

> Man, the most excellent and noble creature of the World, *the principal and mighty work of God, wonder of Nature,* as *Zoroaster* calls him; *audacis naturae miraculum,* as Plato; *the Abridgement and Epitome of the World,* as Pliny; *Microcosmos,* a little world, Sovereign Lord of the Earth, Viceroy of the World, sole Commander and Governor of all creatures in it . . .,

but continues:

> this most noble creature, *Heu tristis & lacrimosa commutatio* (one exclaims) O pitiful change! is fallen from what he was, and forfeited his estate, become *miserabilis homuncio,* a castaway, a caitiff, one of the most miserable creatures of the world, if he be considered in his own nature, as unregenerate man, and so much obscured by his fall that (some few reliques excepted) he is inferior to a beast. . . .[36]

Sir John Davies powerfully expresses the same feeling for Man's miseries:

> I know my body's of so fraile a kinde,
> As force without, feavers within can kill;
> I know the heavenly nature of my minde,
> But tis corrupted both in wit and will.
>
> I know my *Soule* hath power to know all things,
> Yet is she blind and ignorant in all:
> I know I am one of *Natures* litle kings,
> Yet to the least and vilest things am thrall.
>
> I know my life's a paine, and but a span,
> I know my *Sense* is mockt with every thing;
> And to conclude, I know myself a *Man,*
> Which is a *proud* and yet a *wretched* thing.[37]

Yet this view of Man did not detract from the importance of the study of his nature. Renaissance psychology had continuous frontiers on one side with Theology and Moral Philosophy, just as on the other side its borders marched with those of Physiology. In considering sixteenth- and early seventeenth-century ideas of Man it is almost impossible to separate the spheres of the divine, the moralist, the philosopher, the psychologist and the physician. Indeed psychology in the sense in which we understand it can hardly be said to have existed at all; its functions were undertaken as a necessary part of this group of related studies. The study of the nature even of fallen Man was the study of the most God-like thing on Earth, and thus a step to the knowledge of God Himself. It was also a study of the source of Sin and Evil, and the study of spiritual sickness was as much a religious duty as the study of spiritual health. If sin was to be shunned, the first step was to know its origins, which could be physical as well as spiritual. That was why 'Know Thyself' was a watchword among the Elizabethans. The coming of Protestantism intensified the interest in psychology. The more emphasis that was put on the power and responsibility of the individual to redeem himself, the more important became self-knowledge. Milton identifies the Inner Paradise with Order and Harmony in the Soul, and the first step in Samson's redemption is when he regains control of himself and can dispassionately consider his own nature. Whether as the darling of the Universe or its sport, a fraction of the great Unity of Nature or a lone soul fighting for salvation, the proper study of Mankind was Man.

Chapter Two

THE SOUL

THE major difficulty in describing Renaissance psychology is in finding a satisfactory point of departure. The system interlocks in such a way that an explanation of any one part of it depends on an understanding of the rest, and many points raise issues far beyond the scope of this book. It was, to begin with, almost impossible for the Renaissance to consider the soul apart from the body; the theologian might do so, but the physician or the psychologist never. It is in accordance, however, with Renaissance practice to recognize the superior dignity of the Soul by considering it before the body.

The exact nature of the Soul was naturally the subject of much speculation and controversy:

> for the essence and particular knowledge, of all other things it is most hard (be it of man or beast) to discern, as *Aristotle* himself, *Tully*, *Picus Mirandula, Tolet* and other Neoteric Philosophers confess,

says Burton,[1] and it is impossible not to sympathize with the scornful attacks of the Enlightenment on Scholastic discussion of the subject. Even in 1599 Sir John Davies sourly comments:

> Thus these great Clerks their litle wisedom show
> While with their Doctrines they at *Hazard* play,
> Tossing their light opinions to and fro
> To mock the *Lewd*, as learnd in this as they.
>
> For no craz'd braine could ever yet propound
> Touching the *Soule* so vaine and fond a thought,
> But some among these Maisters have bene found,
> Which in their *Schooles* the self same thing have taught.[2]

There was general agreement that the Soul was immaterial, immortal and incorruptible. In some sense or other it existed in the body, and was co-extensive with it. It depended on the body for its knowledge of the outside world, and indeed without the body it could not enter into any relation with the world of sensory experience. On the other hand certain faculties of the Soul—for example, Imagination—apparently extended beyond the confines of the body, and it was generally held that the Rational Soul possessed knowledge not derived from sense. Lemnius sums up the position:

> the Soule doth two waies perfect her faculties; some of them by organs, some without them, and with no help of the body. So, what actions are done by reason and understanding, and judgement of the mind are offices of the soul alone; But manual actions cannot be done without the Ministry of the body.[3]

Although there were believers in Traducianism and in Metempsychosis, it was most usual to hold that a new Soul was created with every living man:

> I think nobly of the soul, and no way approve his opinion,

says Malvolio of Pythagoras.[4] Some held that the Soul was Air, or Fire, or Blood, or a combination of these; some said it was a perfect blend of the Elements, or the Fifth Element; others that it was a refinement of the Spirits or Humours. The orthodox view was that it was a Spirit partaking of the nature of Divinity, which might be regarded as a spark of God in man. It can be observed that although they spoke of the non-corporeal nature of the Soul, many Elizabethans had difficulty in thinking of an immaterial substance. Often they appear to have in mind some kind of extremely rarefied matter—something like the popular idea of ghosts at the present day. The tendency to think of the spiritual as a refined form of the material would follow naturally from the idea of gradation fundamental to the concept of the Great Chain.

Two further views of the Soul which were properly speaking philosophical were of importance to psychology. One was the conception of the Soul as the 'form' of man, that which gave him his character *as* man. Sir John Davies puts this clearly:

> *The Soule a Substance* and a *Spirit* is,
> Which God himselfe doth in the Bodie make,
> Which makes the man, for every man from this
> The *Nature* of a Man and name doth take.[5]

This idea underlay the work of the physiognomers, and was the basis for all attempts to read character from appearance. It was also of importance to neo-Platonism; Spenser refers to it in the *Hymn to Beautie* when he is explaining how it is that beauty of body must imply beauty of soul:

> For of the soule the bodie forme doth take:
> For soule is forme, and doth the bodie make.[6]

Even older was the conception of the Soul as a Harmony, a pattern of the harmony of the Universe. This could be linked with the idea of health as a harmony of the Elements or Humours in the body:

> Proportion causeth harmonie in numbers, in bodies beautie, in humours health, in minde vertue; as contrariwise disproportion, procureth in numbers discord, in bodies deformitie, in humours infirmitie and in the minde vice. . . .[7]

Some authorities divided the Soul into two parts, a Rational part and a 'sensitive' or 'sensual'. It was more usual, however, to speak of the threefold nature of the Soul, although as Burton says

> How these three principal faculties are distinguished and connected . . . is beyond human capacity.[8]

The stock account is given in 'Batman on Bartolome':

> In diverse bodyes the soule is sayde to be three folde, that is to saye, *Vegetabilis*, that giveth lyfe and no feeling, and that is in plants and rootes, *Sensibilis*, that giveth life and feeling, and not reason, that is in unskilfull beastes, *Racionalis* that giveth lyfe, feeling and reason, and this is in men. The Philosopher lykneth the soule that is called *Vegetabilis*, to a Triangle. For as a Triangle hath three corners, this manner soule hath three vertues, of begetting, of nourishing, and of growing. And this soule *Vegetabilis* is like to a Triangle in Geometrie. And hee lykneth the soule *Sensibilis* to a quadrangle square, and foure cornerd. For in a Quadrangle is a line drawne from one corner to another, before it maketh two Triangles; and the soule sensible maketh two triangles of vertues. For wherever the soule sensible is, there is also the soule *Vegetabilis*, but not backwarde. And hee lykeneth the soule *Racionabilis* to a Circle, because of his perfection and conteining.[9]

The three souls were sometimes spoken of as if they were three separate entities—compare Sir Toby's

> Shall we rouse the night-Owle in a catch that will drawe three soules out of one Weaver?[10]

—but they were more commonly regarded as three 'aspects' or 'virtues' of the single soul. Alternatively, and according to the principle of gradation, the Rational soul could be said to embrace the properties of the Vegetable and Sensible souls.[11] The 'ground-plan' of the soul could thus be thought of as a triangle enclosed in a square, which in turn was enclosed in a circle; Spenser so describes the House of Alma:

> The frame thereof seemd partly circulare,
> And part triangulare, O work divine;
> Those two the first and last proportions are,
> The one imperfect, mortall, foeminine;
> Th'other immortall, perfect, masculine,
> And twixt them both a quadrate was the base,
> Proportioned equally by seven and nine;
> Nine was the circle set in heaven's place,
> —All which compacted made a goodly diapase.[12]

The function of the Vegetable soul was to control the basic vital processes of growth, nutrition and reproduction, and it requires little comment. The properties of the Sensible soul, which man shared with brute creation, were much more important and involved. Its two principal faculties were those of Apprehension and Motion, which could be both internal and external. External or 'outward apprehension' was by means of the five senses, upon which the soul depended for its knowledge of the world. The exact mechanism of perception was the subject of much difficulty and speculation; it was bedevilled by the old difficulty as to how far and in what way the senses became assimilated to the object observed. In touching hot things the hand itself became hot, but in what way could the eye be said to become what it saw? It was generally agreed that the senses were passive, and received not the objects themselves, but their 'forms' —a solution obviously full of ambiguities. These forms or 'likenesses' were transferred to the brain by the nerves; the process involved some physical changes, but less in some senses than in others.[13] The senses were in fact ranged in order of merit according to their capacity for receiving form without matter. Touch was the lowest and most bestial of the senses; it has very often a pejorative sense in Shakespeare.[14] After Touch, the order was Taste, Smell, Hearing and finally Sight. Sight, the most dignified of the senses, was the most powerful to stir the passions. This was why 'Action' or rhetorical gesture was of such importance to orators and actors, as Bacon says:

> It is a trivial grammar-school text, but yet worthy a wise man's consideration. Question was asked of Demosthenes, *what was the chief part of an orator?* he answered, *action*: what next? *action*: what next again? *action*. He said it that knew it best, and had by nature himself no advantage in that he commended. A strange thing, that that part of an orator which is but superficial, and rather the virtue of a player, should be placed so high, above those other noble parts of invention, elocution, and the rest; nay, almost alone, as if it were all in all. But the reason is plain. There is in human nature generally more of the fool than of the wise; and therefore those faculties by which the foolish part of men's minds is taken are most potent.[15]

Volumnia echoes this when she advises her son in the art of wooing the public:

> I prythee now, my Sonne,
> Goe to them, with this Bonnet in thy hand,
> And thus farre having stretcht it (here be with them)
> Thy knee bussing the stones: for in such business
> Action is eloquence, and the eyes of th'ignorant
> More learned then the eares. . . .[16]

The passion most easily stirred by the eyes was Love. This hardly needs illustrating: it may suffice to note that in *A Midsummer Night's Dream* the juice of the magic flower is put into their eyes to produce the changeable passions of the lovers. In this context it is important to notice the survival of the belief that the sense of sight was not purely passive, but depended on some kind of ray which issued from the eye, and either impinged on the object and returned to its source, or else acted as a kind of feeler. Donne refers to this belief in *The Ecstasie*:

> Our eye-beames twisted, and did thread
> Our eyes, upon one double thread.[17]

According to this theory, the eyes possessed an 'influence' similar to the 'influence' of the stars—that is, an invisible emanation

c

capable of producing physical effects. This could be used to explain hypnosis, the 'evil eye', and 'fascination', which Cornelius Agrippa explains as:

> a binding, which comes from the spirits of the Witch, through the eyes of him that is bewitched, entering to his heart. Now the instrument of Fascination is the spirit . . . [which] . . . doth alwaies send forth through the eyes, rayes like to itself. . . . So the eye being opened, and intent upon anyone with a strong imagination, doth dart its beames, which are the vehiculum of the spirit, into the eyes of him that is opposite to him, which tender spirit strikes the eyes of him that is bewitched, being stirred up from the heart of him that strikes, and possesseth the breast of him that is stricken, wounds his heart, and infects his Spirit.[18]

The expression 'a piercing eye' had more than a metaphorical significance for the Elizabethan. The same explanation could be offered for love at first sight

> the which hath made some presuppose, that the beames of their eyes, which love incountering with the beames which proceed from the object which inflames them, makes so sweete a mixture, as their union is as it were the fulnesse of al the delights which may be tasted in this life.[19]

The Renaissance, like the Medieval, lover is most often stricken through the eye. In *A Woman Killed with Kindness* Sir Francis Acton, on seeing Susan Mountford for the first time, exclaims:

> Ha, ha, now will I flout her poverty,
> Deride her fortunes, scoffe her base estate;
> My very soule the name of Mountford hate[s].
> But stay; my heart, o what a looke did flye
> To strike my soule through with thy piercing eye.
> I am inchanted, all my Spirits are fled;
> And with one glance my envious spleene strooke dead.[20]

The cluster of thought 'eyes–influence–fascination–witchcraft–love' is of course almost painfully familiar in Elizabethan and Jacobean poetry.

As well as being the most powerful of the Senses, Sight—and this was most relevant in the consideration of Love—was the most liable to err. It was always desirable in case of doubt to check its report by the evidence of one of the other senses. This is why the attempt is made to make ghosts speak, as Hamlet tries to make the ghost of his father, Brutus the ghost of Caesar, and Prince Hal the supposed ghost of Falstaff, and why Macbeth attempts to grasp the visionary dagger. Henry V praises the seeming sobriety of Scroope for

> Not working with the eye, without the eare.[21]

Errors of the Senses were of vital importance, for the Soul itself was blind.

Inward Apprehension was usually ascribed to three powers: Common Sense, Imagination and Memory; but there was considerable variation. It was vulgarly popular to speak of the 'Five Wits', to correspond with the Five Senses, as Shakespeare does on several occasions.[22] The Five Wits were generally said to be Common Sense, Imagination, Phantasy, Estimation and Memory. The division into three powers had, however, the best authority. Strictly speaking the Common Sense was not a separate power, but a combination of all the senses regarded in their common aspect, but it was inevitable that it should come to be treated as independent. Its function was to select and combine the reports of the Five Senses, which themselves could do no more than transmit the impressions made on them. The senses in fact did not know what they perceived, as Sir John Davies says:

> And yet these Porters which all things admit,
> Them selves perceive not, nor discerne the things;
> One *Common* power doth in the forehead sit,
> Which all their proper formes together brings.[23]

It would be Common Sense, for example, which would unite the impressions of roundness, redness, smoothness of skin, and the distinctive qualities of taste and scent to produce the composite 'idea' of 'apple'. Common Sense had also the power to perceive what Aristotle calls 'common sensibles'—that is size, shape, duration, movement, etc.—in the perception of which more than one sense was involved, and also Aristotle's 'incidental sensibles'—that is, qualities associated with certain sense impressions but not directly perceived.[24] This last faculty, however, might more properly be ascribed to the Imagination, or even to the Memory, and there was in fact a great deal of confusion between the three powers of Inward Apprehension. Common Sense had

no power to go beyond the evidence of the senses, and because
of its limited capacity—and still more because of its name—it
soon acquired the meaning of 'the amount of judgement common to all men' and the related meanings of 'the minimum
amount of judgement necessary to existence' and 'innate, untutored wisdom'.[25] In Shakespeare's time the original meaning
was still current, and, indeed, dominant.

The Imagination or Fantasy was a faculty of greater power.
It carried always and most importantly its primary sense of the
ability to perceive mental images, although it was not always in
Elizabethan times, any more than it is to-day, firmly restricted
to that sense. Its first function was to examine the composite
pictures of objects presented by Common Sense, decide their
nature and importance, and to refer their images to the Reason
for judgement, or to the Memory for retention. Although important, it was therefore a subordinate faculty in Man:

> In men it is subject and governed by *reason*, or at least should be;
> but in brutes it hath no superior, and is *ratio brutorum*, all the reason
> they have.[26]

It was, however, particularly apt to rebel against the higher
faculties of the mind. It was able to do this first of all through its
power to arouse the Passions. One of its functions was to decide
on the desirability of objects, that is, their capacity to provide
sensual pleasure. It conveyed its decision to the heart, which was
the seat of the Passions, and the body was thus caused to attempt
to gain a pleasurable object or avoid a source of pain. This immediate judgement required to be supervised by the Reason,
which saw more clearly into the nature of things, but where the
Reason was feeble, or the Passions unduly strong, the Imagination could carry the day, and lead man into ill-considered and
frivolous action. This light judgement was called Fancy, or more
commonly 'Opinion'. Charron says of the Imagination:

> In this part and facultie of the Soul doth opinion lodge, which is a
> vaine, light, crude and imperfect judgement of things drawen from
> the outward senses, and common report, setling and holding it selfe
> to be good in the imagination, and never arriving at the understand-
> ing, there to be examined, sifted and laboured, and to be made reason,
> which is a true, perfect solide judgement of things: and therefore
> it is uncertain, inconstant, fleeting, deceitful, a very ill and dangerous

guide, which makes head against reason, whereof it is a shadow and image, though vaine and untrue. It is the mother of all mischiefs, confusions, disorders: from / it spring all passions, all troubles. It is the guide of fooles, sots, the vulgar sort, as reason of the wise and dexterious.[27]

'Opinion' carried with it the idea of 'popular prejudice', hearsay and 'reputation' in the (unfavourable) Elizabethan sense—in short, Bacon's 'Idols of the Market place'. Since Opinion was an aspect of the Imagination, its characteristic was that it depended purely on the senses, and could judge only by outward show. As Charron says, the 'vulgar sort', whose minds lacked the training to make sounder judgements, were swayed in this way; the Prince of Arragon castigates

> . . . the foole multitude that choose by show,
> Not learning more then the fond eye doth teach;
> Which pries not to th'interior, but like the Martlet,
> Builds in the weather on the outward wall,
> Even in the force and rode of casualtie.[28]

It is significant that the 'temple-haunting martlet' nests on the walls of Glamis, the castle of Deceit. Christ's scornful rejection of the judgement of the 'miscellaneous rabble' in *Paradise Regained*,[29] which has offended many modern readers, is no more than is to be expected from the perfectly rational man. Its fickleness, rashness and its dependence on the evidence of the senses, particularly the eye, connected Fancy or Opinion with light Love. When Friar Laurence hears that Romeo's love for Rosaline has been conquered by a new passion, he comments sadly

> Young men's Love then lies
> Not truly in their hearts, but in their eyes,[30]

and the song which is sung when Bassanio is making his choice of the caskets is a patent warning against reliance on outward appearance:

> Tell me where is fancie bred—
> Or in the heart or in the head:
> How begot, how nourished.   Replie, replie,
> It is engendred in the eyes,
> With gazing fed, and Fancie dies,

> In the cradle where it lies:
>> Let us all ring Fancies knell;
>> Ile begin it. Ding, dong, bell.[31]

True love did not dwell on outward feature, but saw with the heart and to the heart.

The second faculty of the Imagination, and a second source of danger to the Soul, was the power of calling up mental pictures in the absence of an object of sense impression. This power extended not only to memory-images of actual objects: the Imagination could also select and combine images to produce a phantasm which never had or could have an actual existence. This faculty was again not undesirable as long as it remained within the control of the Reason; indeed it was essential to the artist. As soon as the control of the Reason was relaxed, however, the Imagination ran riot. In this way dreams were produced, for in sleep the higher powers of the Soul were withdrawn, and the senses quiescent. Day-dreaming had a similar source; in *The Revenge of Bussy D'Ambois* Clermont thus explains to Guise the appearance of Bussy's ghost:

> 'Twas but your fancy, then, a waking dream:
> For as in sleep, which binds both th'outward senses,
> And the sense common too, th'imagining power
> (Stirr'd up by forms hid in the memory's store,
> Or by the vapours of o'erflowing humours
> In bodies full and foul, and mix'd with spirits)
> Feigns many strange, miraculous images . . .
> So, in the strength of our conceits awake,
> The cause alike doth oft like fictions make.[32]

Although the Elizabethans still believed that dreams might be directly inspired by God, by Angels or by the Devil, they had lost much of the interest in dream lore which Chaucer so markedly evinces. Belief in the hidden significance of dreams was not lost completely (indeed it still survives to-day) but the more scientifically minded tended to take Mercutio's view of

> dreames
> Which are the children of an idle braine
> Begot of nothing, but vain phantasie,[33]

and to seek an explanation in some physical cause,

The Imagination was also responsible for Somnambulism. In the academic play *Lingua*, the Tongue, in pursuit of its aim to be recognized as the sixth sense, makes the other five senses drunk. Somnus appears and charms them to sleep and in their sleep they talk and move about. This is called 'the peripatetic disease' and explained thus:

> the nerves that carry the moving faculties from the braines to the thighs, legs, feet, arms, are wider than the other nerves, wherefore they are not so easily stopt with the vapours of sleep, but are night and day ready to perform what Fancy shall require of them.[34]

This has been called a reminiscence of the sleep-walking scene in *Macbeth*, but could easily have been written independently.

The command of the reason over the imagination tended to be relaxed in illness, and particularly in fever, since heat favoured the working of the fantasy. The drug with which King John is poisoned produces the symptoms of fever, and the Prince says of him:

> Death having praide upon the outward parts
> Leaves them invisible, and his seige is now
> Against the minde, the which he prickes and wounds
> With many legions of strange fantasies,
> Which in their thronge, and presse to that last hold,
> Confound themselves.[35]

The King's ravings are characterized by a wildness of imagery which testifies to the truth of this. The visionary faculty was thus often released in men on the point of death, and they became as 'prophets new-inspired'.[36] Violent passions produced a like effect. The image of the beloved was constantly present to the inward eye of the lover, and the fearful man was tormented by hideous visions. The same result followed on the overthrow of reason by sin. Macbeth, trembling on the verge of murder, sees

> A Dagger of the Minde, a false Creation,
> Proceeding from the heat-oppressed Braine.[37]

Part of the punishment of sinners was the horrible visions projected by their tainted vision. This is in part the reason why the ghosts of their victims so often appear to murderers in Elizabethan drama, as Banquo's ghost does to Macbeth, Caesar's to Brutus, and a whole host to Richard III. Madmen, it hardly needs saying, were those in whom the imagination was so powerful that they were incapable of distinguishing between fantasy and reality.

All in all, the Imagination was a suspect faculty, only to be tolerated if kept in its proper place. Theseus' famous speech in *A Midsummer Night's Dream* has the body of Renaissance opinion behind it:

> Lovers and mad men have such seething braines,
> Such shaping phantasies, that apprehend more
> Then coole reason ever comprehends.
> The Lunaticke, the Lover, and the Poet,
> Are of imagination all compact.
> One sees more divels than vaste hell can hold;
> That is the mad man. The Lover, all as franticke,
> Sees *Helens* beauty in a brow of *Egipt*.
> The Poets eye in a fine frenzy rolling, doth glance
> From heaven to earth, from earth to heaven.
> And as imagination bodies forth the forms of things
> Unknown; the Poets pen turnes them to things
> And gives to airie nothing, a locall habitation,
> And a name. Such tricks hath strong imagination,
> That if it would but apprehend some joy,
> It comprehends some bringer of that joy.
> Or in the night, imagining some feare,
> How easie is a bush suppos'd a Beare?[38]

The Puritan critics of poetry had a strong weapon here, since it could not be denied that poetry was a product of imagination, and the imagination was the mother of lies. This objection could only be met by a distinction, as Puttenham meets it:

> For as the evill and vicious disposition of the braine hinders the sounde judgement and discourse of man with busie & disordered phantasies, for which cause the Greekes call him φανταστικός, so is that part, being well affected, not onely nothing disorderly or confused with any monstruous imaginations or conceits, but very formall, and in his much multiformitie *uniforme*, that is well proportioned, and so passing cleare, that by it, as by a glasse or mirrour, are represented unto the soule all maner of bewtifull visions, whereby the inventive power of the mynde is so much holpen as without it no man could devise any new or rare thing. . . . Wherefore such persons as be illuminated with the brightest irradiations of knowledge and of the veritie and due proportion of things, they are called

by learned men not *phantastici* but *euphantasioti*, and of this sorte of phantasie are all good Poets, notable Captaines stratagematique, all cunning artificers and enginers, all Legislators, Polititiens and Counsellors of estate, in whose exercises the inventive part is most employed, and is to the sound and true judgement of man most needful.[39]

Strictly speaking this argument was a false one, since it claimed for the Imagination a function which was more correctly the property of the Understanding. In practice the Elizabethans most successfully countered this attack by ignoring it.

Motion, the second faculty of the Sensible Soul, was equal in importance to Apprehension. Hamlet brings out the connection between the two faculties:

> Sense, sure, you have,
> Else could you not have motion.[40]

Perception and passion, or desire, were in fact necessary to account for movement, the power which distinguished men and beasts from plants. Properly speaking there were two kinds of movement, Motion and Appetite, perhaps better spoken of as physical and mental motion. Physical motion offers no difficulties; it was merely a question of the correct operation of the nerves and muscles as directed by the Imagination or Reason. Mental motion or Appetite was far more complicated.

There were three kinds of Appetite.[41] The first, Natural Appetite, was the tendency of things to move according to their nature—of heavy bodies, that is, to fall, and of light to rise. Sensitive or Animal Appetite was the power which controlled the vital functions common to man and beast, such as breathing, digestion and the circulation of the blood. It could perhaps be best defined as the power which saw that the right things went to the right places; the blood, for instance, was distributed round the body by natural attraction to the extremities. It was the third kind of Appetite which was of the greatest importance. It was called the Voluntary or Intellective Appetite, because unlike the natural or animal appetites it was, or should be, within the control of the reason.[42] The voluntary appetite was the innate tendency of the soul to seek sensual pleasure and avoid the experience of pain. In order to accomplish this it gave rise to the Passions, which were often spoken of as 'motions'. The passions were on the borderline between mental and physical phenomena;

they were conceived in the mind, but expressed by the body. Thomas Wright says of them:

> These passions then be certain internall actes or operations of the soule, bordering upon reason and sense, prosecuting some good thing, or flying some ill thing, causing therewithall some alteration in the body.[43]

The voluntary appetite contained two complementary 'motions' between which there was a rather fine-drawn distinction. The first—called the 'concupiscible' or 'coveting' appetite—perceived pleasure and pain absolutely, without reference to circumstances. The second—the 'irascible' or 'invading' appetite—perceived the sources of pleasure or pain as accompanied by some difficulty or arduousness. It therefore came to the assistance of the concupiscible appetite, which was not so forceful, and was liable to be daunted by difficulty in obtaining its desires, or by danger from a source of pain.[44] There were various ways of classifying the passions, but it was most usual to follow Aquinas and distinguish eleven, which had their origin in the Concupiscible and Irascible Appetites. If the concupiscible appetite considered a Good in the absolute, without reference to temporal or other conditions, the passion experienced by the soul was Love. If the good was actually present, the passion felt was Joy: if it was in the future, Desire. If an evil was considered absolutely, Hatred was aroused; if the evil was present, Grief, Pain or Sorrow were felt; if it was to come, the emotion experienced was Fear. If a good was contemplated by the irascible appetite as attended by difficulty, the soul felt either Hope or Despair of attaining it. In contemplating a future evil, the irascible appetite gave rise either to Courage or to Despair. If the evil was actually present, Anger was aroused— the only passion without a complementary opposite.[45]

Coeffeteau notes that it was possible for the concupiscible and irascible appetites, which normally worked together, to be in opposition:

> Finally we may observe, that sometimes the Irascible makes us to pursue things which are absolutely contrary to the concupiscible, as when with the hazzard of life (which is so deere and precious to all creatures) we seeke to revenge our selves of a powerfull enemy which hath wronged us.[46]

The hero of Revenge Tragedy was therefore under consider-

able internal as well as external strain; it was no wonder if, like
Hieronymo, he ran mad. A similar stress was put on the soul by
the 'mixed passions', which were compounded of two, possibly
directly opposed, emotions. The most powerful of these were
Envy and Jealousy, which contained a mixture of Love and Hate.
(In Envy, love of the desired object was combined with hatred
of him who possessed it; in Jealousy, love of a possessed object
was combined with hatred of him who wished to take it away.)[47]
Once a man allowed Jealousy to take possession of him, as
Othello does, he was on the high-road to madness. It was finally
possible for the soul to be occupied by two separate and conflict-
ing passions. Perhaps the most common combination would be
grief and anger—again peculiarly appropriate to the revenge
hero, but frequent in all Elizabethan tragedies. Lear is possessed
by grief and anger, and in addition his irascible appetite has
become weakened by age, so that he lacks the force to pursue the
revenge which he desires. The stresses thus set up, aggravated by
his bodily weakness, suffice to overthrow his reason.

The power of the passions to affect and disturb the mind was
recognized in the names 'perturbations' or 'affectations' which
they were also given. It was a commonplace that ' 'Tis Reason's
glory to command affects',[48] but they were known to be unruly
subjects. The rebellion of the subject passions against Reason
their Prince was a favourite theme of academic drama. Jonson
makes extended use of the metaphor in *Every Man in his Humour*:

> Yet can I not but worthily admire
> At natures art: who (when she did inspire
> This heat of life) plac'd Reason (as a king)
> Here in the head, to have the marshalling
> Of our affections: and with soveraignitie
> To sway the state of oure weake emperie.
> But as in divers commonwealthes we see,
> The forme of government to disagree:
> Even so in man who searcheth soone shal find
> As much more varietie of mind.
> Some mens affections like a sullen wife,
> Is with her husband reason still at strife.
> Others, (like proud Arch-traitors that rebell
> Against their soveraigne) practise to expell
> Their liege lord, Reason, and not shame to tread
> Upon his holy and anointed head.[49]

The Passions were, however, not always and unequivocally bad; indeed they were in some degree necessary to the health of soul and body. They were natural to man, and not harmful as long as they were kept in check, as Sir John Davies says:

> Yet were these natural affections good;
> (For they which want them, *blocks* or *divels* be)
> If *reason* in her first perfection stood,
> That she might *Natures* passions rectifie.[50]

Complete absence of passion was a suspect trait; it argued inhumanity. There was considerable distrust of the Stoicism which became fashionable among intellectuals at the close of the sixteenth century:

> we must take heede, that we enter not into that presumptious opinion of many (philosophers) who endevour to leade man to the consideration of dignitie and excellencie, as beeing endued with infinite graces. For they perswade him . . . that by the onely studie of philosophy, he may of himselfe, following his owne nature become maister of al evill passions and perturbations, and attaine to a rare & supreme kind of vertue, which is void of those affections: that being thus exempted and freed from all vice: hee may leade a most happy and perfect life. This did the Stoick philosophers with one consent maintaine and teach. . . .[51]

The stoic refusal to display passion was commonly regarded as merely dissimulation, the vice of which Angelo is guilty. As far as Stoicism preached endurance under the blows of Fate it could be accepted as falling together with the Christian virtue of Patience, but the Stoics committed a grave fault in persuading man that he could by his own unaided effort control his passions:

> Thus whilest they granted to mans power such an excellent and divine disposition, they lift him up in a vain presumption, in pride and trust in himselfe, and in his owne vertue, which in the end cannot but be the cause of his utter undoing.[52]

If man was to learn to control his own passions, it could only be through the assistance of religion. To any attempt to maintain that the ideal soul should never feel the disturbances of emotion there was an unanswerable objection: Holy Writ showed both God and Christ as moved by passion.

The Ideal was the Golden Meane; the watchword 'Temperance'. This is the virtue of which Sir Guyon is the knight, and Spenser makes the lesson clear:

> Then turning to his Palmer said, Old syre
> Behold the image of mortalitie,
> And feeble nature cloth'd in fleshly tyre,
> When raging passion with fierce tyrannie
> Robs reason of her due regalitie,
> And make it servant to her baser part:
> The strong it weakens with infirmitie,
> And with bold furie armes the weakest hart;
> The strong through pleasure soonest falles, the weak
>   through smart.
>
> But temperance, (said he) with golden squire
> Betwixt them both can measure out a meane,
> Neither to melt in pleasures whot desire,
> Nor frie in heartless grief and dolefull teene,
> Thrise happie man, who fares them both atweene . . .[53]

It was the tragedy of the Fall that it made this ideal the harder to achieve, and weakened the sovereign power of the Rational Soul. This, the pinnacle of Man's being, possessed two aspects: the passive power of Wit, and the active power of Will. In popular usage, Wit and Will were often taken as equivalent to Reason and Desire; Shakespeare so uses them several times.[54] Strictly, however, Wit was the power of Intellectual perception, and embraced all the rational faculties. According to Sir John Davies, when the Wit relates and distinguishes objects, it is called Reason, but when it has arrived at the settled truth, it is Understanding. When it is changeable and shifting, it is Opinion; when it is firm and logical, it takes the name of Judgement.[55] In point of fact these terms, with the exception of Opinion, were largely interchangeable. From the exercise of the Understanding comes Knowledge, and from Knowledge, Wisdom. Davies adds a faculty of the Intellectual Memory, which is the repository of wisdom and retains it even after the death of the body.[56]

The function of the Wit was to be the guide of the soul. It received its knowledge of the outside world from the senses, whose reports, collated by Common Sense, were pictured in the Imagination:

> The *wit*, the pupill of the *Soules* clear eye,
> And in mans world the only shining *Starre*;
> Lookes in the mirrour of the phantasie,
> Where all the gatherings of the *Senses* are.[57]

It was distinguished from brute perception first of all by being self-conscious. Secondly, it had the power to see objects in their real nature, and could thus, if healthful and undisturbed, correct errors of the senses and the imagination. (The understanding, for example, knows that the Sun is in fact a very large body and very far off, and not, as the senses might lead us to think, small and quite close.) Wit could also generalize and perceive causal connection, both powers denied to beasts:

> We by our *soules* conceive (as erst was said)
> *Wisdome* and *knowledge* bee'ng incorporal:
> But outward *sense* is altogether stai'd,
> On *qualities* of *things* meere corporall:
> The *soule*, by *reason*, makes *rules* general,
> Of *things* particuler: but *sense* soth goe
> But to *particulers* material;
> The *soule* by th'*effect* the *cause* doth sho,
> But *sense* no more but bare *effectes* doth kno.[58]

This was the 'discourse of reason' which was denied to beasts, who could only judge objects from their appearance and in isolation, and had no powers of logical reasoning.[59] This passage also brings out the difference between Judgement and Opinion. The last particular property of the Wit was the possession of innate ideas:

> Yet hath the *Soule* a dowrie naturall,
> And *sparks of light* some common things to see;
> Not being a *blanck*, where nought is writ at all,
> But what the writer will may written bee:
>
> For nature in mans hart her lawes doth pen;
> Prescribing *truth* to *wit*, and *good* to *will*,
> Which do *accuse*, or else *excuse* all men,
> For every thought, or practice, good or ill.[60]

The line 'Prescribing *truth* to *wit* and *good* to *will*' neatly distinguishes between the two powers. The object of wit was Truth, Wisdom, and ultimately the knowledge of God; the object of will was to obtain that Good which the wit perceived. The Will was also called the 'Rational Appetite', and it pursued Good and avoided Evil just as the Voluntary Appetite pursued pleasure and avoided pain. Hooker makes this plain:

> The object of Appetite, is whatsoever sensible good may be wished for; the object of Will is that good which reason doth lead us to seek . . . neither is any other desire properly termed Will, but that where reason and understanding, or the shew of reason, prescribeth the thing desired.[61]

Hooker's qualification 'or the shew of reason' is an important one. The Will itself was blind, and depended for its knowledge on the Wit. Wit decided the nature of an object, and whether it was morally to be desired or avoided, and Will provided the active drive to carry out this decision:

> And when *wit* is resolv'd, *will* lends her power,
> To execute, what is advisd by *wit*.[62]

The Will was created good and incapable of desiring Evil, but it could be misled by a faulty wit which mistook evil for good. This was so even in unfallen man, as Adam tells Eve:

> But God left free the Will, for what obeyes
> Reason is free, and Reason he made right,
> But bid her well aware, and still erect,
> Least by some faire appeering good surpriz'd
> She dictate false, and misinforme the Will
> To do what God expressly hath forbid.[63]

It was because of the possibility that Evil might disguise itself as Good, mislead the Wit and so lead the Will into sin, that hypocrisy and deceit were so abominable to the Elizabethans.

The passions distorted the perceptive power and prevented the judgement from perceiving the true nature of things; they also stimulated the Imagination to keep the image of the desired object constantly before the eye of the Understanding.[64] In fallen man the Will itself might become corrupt, because it had a certain 'sympathy' with the Sensitive Appetite:

> Moreover the Will, by yeelding to the Passion, receyveth some little bribe of pleasure, the which moveth her, to let the bridle loose, unto inordinate appetites, because she hath ingrafted in her, two inclina-

tions, the one to follow Reason, the other to content the Sences; and this inclination (the other beeing blinded by the corrupt judgement, caused by inordinate Passions) here she feeleth satisfied.[65]

A fundamentally corrupted Will would take command of the Reason, and induce what we should call 'rationalization' or 'wishful thinking':

and for this cause she commandeth the witte to employ all the power and force, to finde out reasons and perswasions that all the appetite demaundeth, standeth with reason and is lawfull; the which collusion, I take to be one of the rootes of all mischiefes that nowe cover the face of / the worlde, that is, a wicked will commanding the wit, to find out reasons to pleade for Passions . . .[66]

This recalls the 'motive-hunting' Iago.

A mind in which the Will was perverted was corrupt in all its powers. Coeffeteau explains that the passions of an evil soul cannot be good:

So we see both good and bad, feare, desire and rejoice alike. But the wicked have bad feares, wicked desires, and bad joyes, whereas the good have none but good feares, good desires, and good joyes, for that the branches do alwaies participate of the nature of the roote.[67]

Satan's virtues in *Paradise Lost*—they are the virtues of a warrior chieftain, far removed from 'patience and Heroick Martyrdom' —are therefore not virtues at all; they are poisoned at their source. Nor could the possession of one good quality redeem an otherwise evil character: indeed in some ways it aggravated its evil. To the Renaissance, Passion could never be its own justification, as to some extent it has become since the Romantic period. Anthony's is a case of a perverted Will, which knows it is pursuing evil, but cannot draw back:

> I must from this enchanting Queene breake off,
> Ten thousand harmes, more than the illes I know
> My idlenesse doth hatch—

but

> I'the east my pleasure lies.[68]

Garzoni, in *The Hospitall of Incurable Fooles*, includes under the heading 'Amorous Fooles', Mark Anthony:

who besotted with the love of *Cleopatra* Queene of Egypt, lost for her onely cause both his empire, life and honour.[69]

This of course is not to deny that Shakespeare makes the love of Anthony and Cleopatra splendid, moving, and (to Cleopatra at least) eventually ennobling, but the moral judgement is present in his play, even if it is not emphasized. *Anthony and Cleopatra* is perhaps more 'the tragedy of Anthony' than we think, and perhaps in a slightly different sense. It is not until the Restoration that we come to '*All for Love: or the World Well Lost*'.

Macbeth's will becomes perverted in the course of his tragedy, until the logic of events forces him into a position where his Reason is persuaded there is no escape except through further crime:

> I am in blood
> Stept in so farre, that should I wade no more,
> Returning were as tedious as go o'er.[70]

Richard, Edmund and Iago—each dominated in varying degrees by the passions of Ambition, Envy and Revenge—are so perverted that Evil has in fact become their Good. They can justify their villainy rationally, and even jest about it; they recognize no moral standard but expediency, and no higher power than their own Will. They are in a sense worse than Satan, for he at least recognizes the existence of a Good which he has lost. Shylock is a less magnificent villain, but even he uses his reason to justify the sin of Usury. (Wright actually cites Usurers among those who make use of Reason to attack Christianity: Usury was a form of Atheism.[71]) These men were horrible examples of the power of the Soul to turn against its Creator.

Man was not powerless against the onslaughts of passion and vice. He could first of all develop his self-control, and by taking pains acquire the virtues of Temperance and Continence. He could learn to know himself, and where the chief sources of danger lay for him, and so avoid temptation. He could even employ one passion to drive out another, or find some other means to distract his soul from the pursuit of its own ruin. But his most powerful defence against Sin was Conscience, God's voice in man. In *The Purple Island*, Fletcher represents Conscience as a handmaid attending on Voletta, the Will, the consort of Prince Reason:

E

On her a royall damsel still attends,
And faithful Counseller, *Synteresis*;
For though *Voletta* ever good intends,
Yet by fair ills she oft deceived is:
        By ills so fairly drest with cunning slight,
        That Vertue's self they well may seem to sight,
But that bright Vertues self oft seems not half so bright.

Therefore *Synteresis* of nimble sight,
Oft helps her doubtfull hand, and erring eye;
Els mought she ever stumbling in this night
Fall down as deep as deepest *Tartarie*:
        Nay thence a sad-fair maid, *Repentance*, rears,
        And in her arms her fainting Lady bears,
Washing her often stains with ever-falling tears.[72]

To Shakespeare, as to the Elizabethans in general, Conscience
was the power which smote the Soul with remembrance of past
misdeeds and with fear of punishment to come. The torments
of Conscience were Sin's punishment on Earth; not even so
hardened a villain as Richard III can escape them:

O coward conscience! how dost thou afflict me?
The lights burne blew. It is now dead midnight.
Cold fearefull drops stand on my trembling flesh. . . .
My conscience hath a thousand severall Tongues,
And every Tongue brings in a severall Tale,
And everie Tale condemnes me for a Villaine;
Perjury in the highest degree;
Murther, sterne murther, in the dyr'st degree,
All severall sinnes, all us'd in each degree,
Throng to 'th'Barre, crying all, Guilty, Guilty.
I shall dispaire, there is no creature loves me;
And if I die, no soule shall pittie me:
Nay, wherefore should they? Since that I my Selfe
Finde in my Selfe, no pittie to my Selfe.[73]

To fall into Despair, the deadly sin of *Tristitia* with which the
Red Cross Knight is tempted,[74] wherein the Soul loses faith in
the infinite mercy of God, would be a crime worse than any
which Richard has committed. The true function of the Conscience was to call the soul to Repentance, the high-road to the
Mercy of God.

Manye been the weyes espirituels that leden folk to oure Lord Iesu Crist, and to the regne of glorie. / Of which weyes, ther is a ful noble wey and a ful convenable, which may nat faile to man ne to womman, that thurgh sinne hath misgoon fro the righte wey of Jerusalem celestial; / and this wey is cleped Penitence,[75]

says the Parson, and devotes his Tale to an elaboration of the theme. True Penitence cannot fail, but it must be whole-hearted, as Claudius realizes.[76] The dramatic point of the Prayer Scene lies in the fact that Claudius cannot repent, largely because he is not prepared to give up the fruits of his crime; Hamlet, however, believes him to be in a state of grace, and concludes that to kill him would be to rescue his soul from perdition and reward him with eternal felicity.

It was never forgotten that the Soul was a portion of Divinity in Man, and that its Creator would not abandon it as long as it showed a desire to be reunited with Him. Since the Fall, it was only by Divine Grace that Man could maintain the Divine order within his being. It might be, as most Catholics believed, that the intervention of Grace was continuously necessary to enable man to overcome his unruly Passions. Protestants on the other hand—and the most notable example in our context is Milton— held that it was open to Man through Divine Mercy to regain the supremacy of the Reason and attain the Inner Paradise with its aid. One of the lessons of *Samson Agonistes* is that even if one of the Elect falls through passion, he may regain Salvation by means of repentance, self-knowledge, patience and fortitude. The infinite Mercy of God might be extended to the sinner even in the last moment; perhaps only Satan and his followers were irretrievably damned.

Chapter Three

THE BODY

SINCE the Soul and the body were so closely connected, and the Soul had such need of the body as an instrument for the execution of its wishes, the consideration of the nature and structure of the body was an essential part of the psychologist's task. By 1600, of course, considerable advances had been made in the science of Anatomy, and the authority of the Ancients had been seriously challenged. We cannot but feel surprised that these discoveries were not more quickly accepted and their implications sooner realized. It seems ridiculous to us that men should have continued to maintain that the thigh-bone was curved, or that man possessed an inter-maxillary bone, because Galen had said so, when Vesalius had demonstrated the falsity of both assertions. We must remember that natural conservatism was strengthened both by the comparatively slow diffusion of knowledge and by the tremendous prestige of the old authorities. To-day a new discovery is promulgated almost overnight, and we are so accustomed to scientific advance that we assume that what is new must be correct. The temper of the Renaissance was different; it was prepared for new hypotheses to be advanced, but it was not prepared to accept them at sight. Even in the seventeenth century it was at least a generation before Harvey's discovery of the circulation of the blood was fully accepted; it is more striking still to find 'the Copernican *hypothesis*' listed by Sprat among the topics discussed by the new Royal Society. The anatomy which we must discuss, therefore, was a curious blend of old tradition and new discovery; fortunately we do not need to investigate it in great detail.

Several methods of classifying the parts of the body were in use at Shakespeare's time. Perhaps the most common—and probably the most suitable for us to follow—began by dividing

the body first of all into *Parts containing* and *Parts contained*.[1]
Parts containing consisted of two subdivisions. The first of these
was *Similar Parts*—that is, parts which could be divided a number of times and still retain the same nature. Bones, gristle, liga-
ments, membranes and 'strings' (or fibres) all belonged to this
category; they were regarded as developing in the foetus from
the seed of the father, and were therefore sometimes called
'spermatic parts'. Fat, flesh and skin were Similar parts produced
from the blood of the mother, and were thus 'sanguine parts'.
The last group of *Similar Parts* were the veins, arteries, nerves
and sinews, the last two terms being interchangeable. These
were all thought of as hollow tubes or pipes, and served to carry
the *Parts contained*.

The second sub-division of *Parts containing* were the *Dissimilar
parts*, also called 'organical' or 'instrumental' parts. These were in
turn divided into *Outward parts*—the limbs, features and so on—
and *Inward parts* or organs. The most important of the outward
parts was the Face, because it most fully expressed the nature of
the Soul. The Inward Parts were usually considered to form three
regions, each dominated by a principal organ.[2] The first of these
regions was that of the Lower Belly, of which the principal
organ was the Liver. This was the region of the Vegetable functions, principally of Nutrition, of which there were four phases:
attraction, concoction (or digestion), retention and evacuation.
The Middle Belly was the seat of the Vital functions, particularly
respiration and the maintenance of vital heat. Its principal
organ was the Heart. Lastly came the Head, which contained
only one organ, the Brain. There was some tentative attempt
to localize the mental faculties. Generally the forepart of
the brain was regarded as the place of Common Sense, the
middle part of Imagination, and the hinder part of Memory.
Sometimes the front of the brain was said to be divided into
three ventricles: the left and right ventricles received the reports
of the senses, and the Common sense resided between them and
combined their messages.[3]

> Liver, Braine and Heart,
> Those soveraigne thrones,[4]

were the essential organs without which life was impossible.
The Brain as the seat of Reason was naturally the most noble,

but the Heart was in some ways the most important. According to Burton, it is

> the seat and fountain of life, of heat, of spirits, of pulse and respiration; the Sun of our body, the King and sole commander of it; the seat and organ of all passions and affections; (*primum vivens ultimum moriens;* it lives first, and dies last, in all creatures). . . .[5]

The parallel with the Sun was very frequent. Henry V says to Katherine:

> a good Heart, *Kate*, is the Sunne and the Moone, or rather the Sunne, and not the Moone; for it shines bright, and never changes, but keepes his course truly.[6]

There was a correspondence between the Heart's function of maintaining vital heat in the body and the Sun's diffusion of 'genial warmth' over the Earth. The Heart's most important role was as the seat of the Passions.

Parts contained were the three Spirits and the four Humours. The Vegetable, Vital and Animal Spirits were the media through which the threefold Soul carried out its operations in the body, and were thus the essential link between the spiritual and the material in Man. Some, indeed, claimed that the Soul was in fact nothing else than the three spirits, but this was not generally accepted. Both the spirits and the humours were produced in the liver by the 'concoction of food.'[7] Strictly speaking this was the 'second concoction'; the first was in the stomach where the nutritious part of the food was extracted and passed on to the Liver as 'chylus' which is described as 'a substance like unto Almond Butter'.[8] From the chylus the liver extracted Blood, Vegetable spirits and the Humours. 'Lily-livered' was thus synonymous with 'cowardly', for if no blood was found in the liver, its source, there could be little elsewhere in the body.[9] There was a third concoction, which was the absorption of the blood and humours by the parts of the body to which they were distributed.[10]

The spirits were thought of as very pure, rarefied and volatile substances. Lowe says of them:

> they are a substaunce subtill and aerious of our bodie, bredde of the part most pure and thinne of the blood, sent through all the bodie, to the effect, the members may doe their proper actions.[11]

They were of a 'simple' nature: that is, all of one substance and indivisible. From the Liver, the Vegetable spirits passed along the veins with the blood, and enabled the Vegetable Soul to carry out its functions. When they reached the heart they were transformed into Vital spirits. The right ventricle of the heart received blood from the liver and sent some of it to nourish the lungs. Of the rest, the thinner and more 'subtle' part filtered through into the left ventricle, where it was mixed with air. The heart drew air from the lungs partly for this purpose, and partly to maintain a correct temperature in the body. The contraction of the heart drew blood, spirits and air to it; its expansion sent them forth again, and also expelled the 'sooty excrements' with which the lungs and heart might otherwise be choked.[12] Systole and diastole were controlled by the fibres or 'heart-strings', which are several times used by Shakespeare as a symbol for the essential life of the body.[13] The Vital spirits were distributed throughout the body by the arteries, which were

> formed for the conveyance of that more sprightly bloud which is elaborate in the heart. This bloud is frothy, yellowish and full of spirits.[14]

The chief office with which the Vital spirits were charged was the maintenance of vital heat in the body, as Crooke says:

> this spirit cherisheth the inbred heat of every part, quickens it when it becommeth drowsie, bringeth it forth when it lyes hid, and being spent or wasted, restoreth it again.[15]

Since life itself depended on the maintenance of vital heat, this office of the spirits was of the highest importance; if they failed in this task the result could only be death.

Some of the Vital spirits were brought by the arteries to the brain, where they were further rarefied and made still more subtle. The centre of this operation was held to be the 'rete mirabile', later known as the 'circle of Willis'.[16] In this way were produced the Animal Spirits, whose chief function was to make possible the operations of the Sensible Soul—motion and apprehension. (The name 'animal' is of course derived from 'anima'.) The centre of the 'motive power' was in the brain, and its messages were carried by the animal spirits along the nervous system to the muscles. It was thus that a person of quick and boisterous movements could be said to be 'full of animal spirits'. Anthony refers to this in his boast:

> though gray
> Do somthing mingle with our yonger brown, yet ha'we
> A Braine that nourishes our Nerves . . .[17]

In mental motion (i.e. the Passions) it was the animal spirits which caused the heart to induce whatever physical reactions were appropriate to the passion experienced.[18]

In Sensation the animal spirits had a more complicated role to play. It was they who transferred the image of an object from the pupil of the eye to the Imagination. Others held that it was the animal spirits which issued from the eyes and formed the eyebeams. It is probably this conception which underlies Troilus' reference to the eye as 'that most pure spirit of sense' which in comparison to Cressida's hand is 'hard as palm of ploughman'.[19] Hearing was produced by the 'rebounding' of air on the ear-drum, and the effects of this were again passed on to the brain by the spirits. In these two senses the spirits acted as an inter-mediary between the object and the brain, and the object itself produced no material effect—in fact all the senses themselves re-ceived was an 'impression' on the air. These senses were there-fore purer than the rest. In Smell a 'smoke' was drawn in from the object, mixed with the spirits and so actually penetrated the brain itself. Consequently the brain was refreshed and delighted by sweet vapours and corrupted by foul air, which bred disease. Similarly the tongue (which was hollow) sucked in 'humours' from the object, and these or their 'likeness' were carried by the spirits up to the brain. In touch the skin (and especially the skin of the hand) became itself hot or cold or damp, and the spirits, which were distributed to the surface of the body by numberless small nerves, transferred these sensations. It was rather less clear how exactly the skin received the impression of roughness or hardness, and so on, but again it was the nerves which carried these impressions.[20]

The importance of the spirits and their dual nature as a bridge between the material and mental,—in which they resembled the passions,—is expressed by Donne in *The Extasie*:

> As our blood labours to beget
> Spirits, as like soules as it can,

Because such fingers need to knit
That subtile knot which makes us man:

So must pure lovers soules descend
T'affections and to faculties,
Which sense may reach and apprehend,
Else a great Prince in prison lies.[21]

The 'great Prince' is both Love, which must be expressed physically even though it is a spiritual experience, and the Soul, which must express itself in the body through the medium of the spirits. Since the maintenance of vital heat and both sense and motion depended on the spirits, their efficiency was a matter of the greatest importance. As both blood and air entered into their composition, they were easily affected by physical conditions. Lack of food, for example, would mean that insufficient blood would be 'concocted'; the spirits would therefore be feeble, and the Soul's command over the body relaxed. Extreme cold would numb the spirits so that the sufferer became dull and drowsy, and it might eventually overcome vital heat. Heavy or impure air would clog and corrupt the spirits. Suffocation resulted when a complete deprivation of air prevented the heart from 'elaborating' spirits altogether. The spirits were quickly exhausted by mental or by physical labour, and by violent passion. It was also possible to suffer from a congenital weakness or 'lowness' of the spirits. At the same time the very rarefied nature of the spirits meant that they were very sensible to intangible influences. Lorenzo comments on the power of music over the spirits—a power ultimately connected with the conception of the soul as harmony.[22] Fascination or enchantment has already been noted as a domination by the spirits of the witch over the spirits of the victim. Prospero 'binds up' Ferdinand's spirits 'as in a dreame'; his 'nerves are in their infancie againe / and have no vigour in them'.[23] The use of 'spirit' in many contexts quickly shaded off into the modern meanings of 'courage' or 'morale', but in essence to 'be in good spirits' meant that the Soul had full command of the body, and was able to use it freely to express her own nature.

The Humours were also formed in the liver from the Chylus by the 'second concoction'. They were of a grosser and in a special sense more 'elemental' nature than the Spirits. They were often spoken of as 'the children of the elements'; each humour corresponded to an element, and possessed the same two primary qualities as its element possessed. Thus Blood, like Air, was hot and moist; Choler, like Fire, hot and dry; Phlegm, like Water, cold and moist; and Melancholy, like Earth, was cold and dry.[24] Each humour derived from an element in food and had a special affinity with the parts of the body in which that element predominated. Lowe defines a Humour as

> a thinne substance, into the which our nourishment is first converted, or it is an naturall *Jus* that the bodie is intertained, norished or conserved with,[25]

and Batman gives us an account of how the humours were 'distilled' by concoction out of the different kinds of food:

> first working heate turneth what is colde and moyst into the kind of fleme, and then what is hot and moyste into the kinde of bloud: and then what is hot and drye into the kinde of *Cholera*: and then what is colde and drye into the kinde of *Melancholia*. Then the processe is such first, fleame is bread, as an humour half sod: second bloud, that is perfectly sodde: the third *Cholera*, that is over sodde: the last is *Melancholia*, that is more earthly, and the dregges of the other.[26]

From the liver the humours passed along the veins with the blood, in which they were mingled. Although the sanguine humour often usurped the name of 'blood' it was in fact like the other humours only a constituent of it. The humours could be distinguished if blood were drawn from the body and left to stand:

> And as there are foure elements of which our bodies are compounded, so there are foure sorts of humours answerable to their natures, being all mingled together with the blood; as we may see by experience in blood let out of ones body. For uppermost we see as it were a little skum like to the floure or working of new wine, or of other wine when it is powred forth. Nexte we may see as it were small streames of water mingled with the blood. And in the bottome is seene a blacker and thicker humor, like to the lees of wine in a wine vessel.[27]

The first humour that becomes visible is choler, the next phlegm and the third melancholy: 'blood' forms the remainder. A physician could tell which humour predominated in the blood by looking at it or tasting it. Ambroise Paré says that Blood is 'indifferent' (or average) in density, red, rosy or crimson in colour, and sweet to the taste. Choler is thin, yellow or pale, and bitter. Phlegm is liquid, white and 'unsavoury' (i.e. tasteless); Melancholy is gross and muddy, blackish and sour and biting to the palate.[28]

By 1600 the original humoral theory had become very considerably extended and complicated. Lemnius, for example, lists four kinds of phlegm: sweet, which induces drowsiness; sour, which causes hunger; salt, which produces fever and 'tetters' (or scabs); and glassy, which was extremely cold and caused 'stoppages' in the body—e.g. constipation.[29] The other humours could be similarly subdivided. A further complication was the introduction of 'unnatural,' 'naughty' or 'corrupt' humours. The theory was that humours could change their nature by 'adustion' or 'putrefaction', a process by which they burned up and became sour, like wine when it turns to vinegar:

> those humours are against nature, which being corrupted, infect the body and the parts in which they are contained, retaining the names and titles of the humours, from whose perfection they have revolted; they all grow hot by putrefaction, although they were formerly by their own nature cold.[30]

Thus Lemnius recognizes two kinds of natural choler, and no fewer than six kinds of choler adust—'pale' or 'citrine', 'yolky', 'leek green', 'rusty' or 'brassy', 'blueish' and 'black'.[31] This process of adustion was analogous to the process of 'seething' by which the four humours were originally formed in the liver, and like that process (and unlike the circular changing of the elements) it could only go one way. All corrupt humours, that is, tended towards melancholy, and in fact were often spoken of as 'melancholic', which was a pregnant source of confusion. It was possible to speak, for example, of 'melancholy of choler adust' and so on, and this greatly widened the scope of the term. Humours could become adust by themselves, or when mixed with other humours. Thus, according to Langton, choler adust was 'black and biting', but if it 'putrefied' when mixed with thick phlegm, the result was 'yolkie choler'; if with thin phlegm, then 'pale or citrine' choler was produced.[32] The humoral theory was in fact being extended to cover all the natural and morbid secretions of the body. Fortunately the finer distinctions were of little concern to the psychologist, although all unnatural humours were in some degree dangerous to the health and would thus tend to affect the balance of the mind.

The humours had various functions to perform in the body. They brought nourishment, for example, to those parts of the body similar in nature to themselves. Thus melancholy fed the cold and dry parts, such as the bones, while phlegm nourished the cold and moist parts, such as the brain and marrow, and also lubricated all moving parts—the joints, for instance, and the tongue. Blood brought nourishment to all the body, but especially to the sanguine parts, for which it had an affinity. Choler and melancholy aided in digestion: choler by 'sharpening' the appetite and the expulsive power, and the thick melancholy by assisting in the retention of food in the stomach.[33] It is obvious that these humours would need to be present only in the correct amounts, for otherwise digestive disorders would arise, with repercussions on the general health of the body. The amount of each of these humours in the body was controlled by a special organ which drew off and purged any excess, maintaining a reserve which could be called on if needed. The controlling organ for choler was the gall-bladder, which thus naturally became a symbol of bitterness, anger and also courage.[34] The organ of melancholy was the spleen, but it is not till much later than this period that 'a fit of the spleen' came to be used for a mood of depression. In Shakespeare's time the spleen was on the contrary regarded as the seat of laughter. The reason for this must be that it was responsible for what we (and the Elizabethans) would call 'good humour', since if it failed in its duties the body would become flooded with melancholy. 'Spleen' did however have the sense of bad temper or arrogance; the transference probably comes through the phrase 'a merry spleen', meaning a whim or caprice, and so a fit of petulance.[35]

An excess of any humour would throw the body out of balance, and so would a deficiency, for the different humours kept each other in check. Thus the cold melancholy acted as a 'bridle' to the hot humours of blood and choler, and if not enough was present in the blood, the body would suffer an 'intemperature'. Ideally the humours should be in perfect balance, but this condition was seldom or never found.[36] In the ordinary, averagely well-balanced man the proportion of the humours fluctuated according to his age, the time of day, the season of the year and so on. Walkington, in *The Opticke Glasse of Humours*, has a circular diagram which equates each humour not only with an element, but further with a time of life, a season, a wind, a planet, and with three signs of the Zodiac. Thus choler, besides corresponding to fire, is paralleled by Youth, Summer, the West Wind, Mars, and the constellations Aries, Leo and Sagittarius. Blood corresponds to Air, Adolescence, Spring, the South Wind, Jupiter, the Gemini, Libra and Aquarius. Melancholy corresponds with Old Age, Winter, the North Wind, Saturn, Cancer, Scorpio and Pisces. The parallels to phlegm are Middle Age, Autumn, the South-east Wind, the Moon, Taurus, Virgo and Capricornus. This means in other words that choler, for example, tends to predominate in the body during Youth, or in the Summer, and when Mars is in the ascendant and so on. Each humour tended also to dominate in the body at a particular time of day: blood from 3 a.m. to 9 a.m.; choler from 9 a.m. to 3 p.m.; phlegm from 3 p.m. to 9 p.m.; and melancholy from 9 p.m. to 3 a.m.[37] Sometimes the last two periods are reversed, and so also are some of Walkington's last two sets of correspondences, so that melancholy is associated with Autumn and so on. In most men one humour tended to predominate all the time, so that they could be said to be of a sanguine, choleric, phlegmatic or melancholic 'complexion'. In moderation such a predominance was not dangerous, provided that the condition was recognized, and care was taken to see that it did not become aggravated. It was impossible to say at what point a tendency towards the predominance of a particular humour became a settled 'intemperature' or where the boundary lay between safety and danger. Any deviation from the norm of perfect balance was in some degree an illness, and because of this, and also because physical conditions could radically alter the constitution of the body in such a way as to produce what we as well as the Renaissance would call 'temperament', Elizabethan psychological writers had to take into account everything which had an effect on man's physical nature. In this reckoning the first group of factors was Heredity, Sex and Age.

The transference of hereditary characteristics was naturally very puzzling to the scientists of the Renaissance. The physical bond between parents and children was very close, since it was generally held, following Aristotle, that the child was formed of the seed of the father and the blood of the mother, the seed providing the form and the catamenia, the matter.[38] Other writers insisted that the 'seed' of the mother also played a vital part, and that in fact it depended on circumstance whether the paternal seed provided the form and the maternal seed the matter, or vice versa.[39] Some believed that there must also be a kind of invisible secretion from every part of the father to account for the detailed physical resemblances often found between father and child. This theory—pangenesis—is spoken of by Crooke, however, as 'that old errour' and as 'a beggarly rudiment received from hand to hand among the Auntients'.[40] However the mysteries of procreation were to be explained, it was clear that children did in fact inherit physical and mental characteristics from their parents. The power of the soul over the body was illustrated by pre-natal influence. There is still a rural superstition that 'hare-lip' is produced if a pregnant woman is startled by a hare running across her path, and other deformities could be explained in a similar way. If during conception and gestation the woman's imagination dwelt lovingly on the image of a man (be he her husband or another) the child would bear his likeness; the resemblance of a posthumous child to his father could be caused in this way.[41] 'Temperature' could be directly transferred from parent to child. Children of old men, for example, would be weak and feeble, because of their father's cold and dry complexion, but they might also be exceptionally intelligent—another belief still current to-day.[42] Conception during the menstrual period was to be avoided, for at that time the woman's body was flooded with 'corrupt' humour, and the child would be born deformed and unhealthy.[43]

Huarte, who subscribes to the view that the woman's seed plays an important part in the formation of the embryo, provides a more elaborate and 'scientific' account of the transference of temperature. The woman's seed, he says, is naturally cold and moist, and needs to be qualified by the hot and dry seed of the man. Couples should therefore be correctly matched so that their seeds are complementary; if a woman is cold and moist 'in the third degree', for example, she should marry a man who is very hot and dry. The ideal is to approach as nearly as possible to a perfect balance. If the husband's seed is too fierce, the child will be of a choleric complexion: if on the other hand the husband's seed is insufficiently hot and dry, the child will be weak, phlegmatic and effeminate. In such a case the husband should attempt to heat and dry his seed by proper exercise and diet. Huarte explains in this way why bastard children, such as Edmund and Faulconbridge, are 'ordinarily deliver, coragious and very advised'. For

> a man . . . who goeth seeking a woman not his owne, is replenished with this fruitful, digested and well seasoned seed;

consequently his seed qualifies that of the woman, dominates it and forms the child, while her seed provides the 'nourishment' of the embryo, and this is the correct procedure. Married men are apt to beget children when their seed is weak and not properly digested, so that lawful children are often formed by the mother's seed and are in consequence cold, moist and 'unable'.[44] Huarte's advice to parents is all devoted to the successful procreation of men-children; he has of course no doubt that sons are far preferable to daughters.

It was realized that all the complexities of heredity could not be explained. Nevertheless, it was strongly felt that children ought to resemble their parents, and particularly their father, and there was something suspicious, if not actually evil, in a child who did not. Moreover, since children were so closely linked physically with their parents—literally of their blood—rebellion by children was a horrifyingly unnatural thing. Goneril and Regan's conduct does not merely grieve and anger Lear, it frightens him. It is an offence against the laws of Nature, almost as if his own body had turned against itself. With this was connected the idea that children should respect and obey their parents as part of the natural order of the Universe. The father was head of the family as the King was head of the state, and should be accorded the same obedience. Brabantio and Capulet are not merely domestic tyrants whose dignity has been affronted; they represent a principle which has been flouted. Henry IV is offended both as a King and as a father by the Prince's unfilial conduct in taking the crown. Paternal affection, at any rate in theory, was not so much a matter of tenderness as of Justice, and should be extended to children only in so far as they merited it.

Lear is doubtless too hasty when he casts off Cordelia for failing, as he thinks, to show him proper respect, but he could claim to be acting justly in cursing Goneril and Regan. The fact that several writers rather go out of their way to point out that unreasoning parental fondness is a weakness, however, rather suggests that Elizabethan fathers and mothers were less strict in practice than in theory, although we should no doubt think most of them unduly severe with their children. In this, as in so much else, the Elizabethans would certainly invoke the principle of the Golden Mean.

The effect of Sex on constitution and character was relatively simple. By nature women tended towards the phlegmatic or cold and moist temperament, and for that reason their bodies were more fleshy, softer and weaker than men's. Their hair also was longer and thicker, their eyes larger and more moist, their voices softer, and their faces paler and more delicate in colour. The preponderance of water in their composition meant that they dissolved more easily into tears than men. They were also subject to sudden rages, since their

> flesh is loose, soft and tender, so that the choler being kindled, presently speads all the body over, and causeth a sudden boyling of the blood about the heart.[45]

Their anger was soon over, however, for they lacked the natural heat to maintain it, and they were usually weak and cowardly. They were in fact inferior beings, 'imperfect men'; their lack of vital heat restricted their mental as well as their physical powers, as Lemnius says:

> also I ascribe to this, that a woman is not so strong as a man, not so wise and prudent, nor hath so much reason, nor is so ingenious in contriving her affairs as a man is.[46]

A woman therefore needed to be sustained and guided by her natural master; Milton was by no means unique in his views on the proper relation of the sexes. All this, of course, did not preclude the accounts of woman's guile, treachery, inborn viciousness and desire to dominate which have been commonplaces of anti-feminism since the time of the early Fathers.

Men should by nature tend to heat and dryness, and were therefore stronger than women, braver, more intelligent, more magnanimous and so on. It was realized, however, that great variations were possible in the temperament of men—more apparently than in the case of women, unless it is merely that psychologists paid greater attention to the more important animal. There was, however, a strong desire to keep the characteristics of the two sexes distinct. It might be possible to feel some admiration for masculine women such as Mary Ambree, Moll Frith, or (in an idealized shape), Britomart. Since Man was the superior being it was creditable in these women to have acquired elements of his nature. Such creatures were, nevertheless, exceptional; the virago was a prodigy and needed, like Katherine the Shrew, to be brought as soon as possible to a proper state of mind. It was no virtue in a man to possess any feminine quality, except possibly tenderness and affection for his friends. The effeminate man, if not actually vicious, was at best a poor thing. Tamburlaine rails against his sons when he thinks them possessed of a 'temperament' more appropriate to the opposite sex:

> But yet me thinks their looks are amorous,
> Not martiall as the sons of *Tamburlaine*.
> Water and ayre being simbolised in one
> Argue their want of courage and of wit,
> Theire haire as white as milke and soft as Downe,
> Which should be like the quilles of Porcupines,
> As blacke as Jeat, and hard as Iron or steel,
> Bewraies they are too dainty for the wars.
> Their fingers made to quaver on a Lute,
> Their armes to hang about a Ladies necke:
> Their legs to dance and caper in the aire:
> Would make me thinke them Bastards, not my sons,
> But that I know they issued from thy wombe,
> That never look'd on man but *Tamburlaine*.[47]

Age had a powerful effect on temperament. It was customary to divide Man's life, as Jaques does, into seven ages, although there were variations in the precise divisions. Thomas Wright gives a schematic division into seven groups of seven years or multiples of seven years. From birth to 7 years is the age of Infancy; 7 to 14, that of Childhood; 14 to 21, Adolescence. Youth extended from the 21st to the 28th year; Manhood from the 28th to the 49th; Old Age from the 49th to the 63rd. The

E

63rd year, being the product of the magic numbers 7 and 9 was
the Grand Climacteric; thereafter to 70, the Biblical span, or to
77, a man was in the realms of Senility.[48] The qualities of youth
were Heat and Moisture. As life progressed these vital qualities became wasted, until the body at last lay cold and dry in
death.

> Our life is, as it were a certain progress to drieness, which when it
> comes to the height consequently causeth death,

says Paré.[49] It followed that the characteristic humour of youth
was the sanguine, which disposed young men to Love and
Generosity, but also to a certain levity of mind. Grown men were
of a drier, more choleric nature, and therefore made better
soldiers and poets. Old men first became subject to phlegm; as
the 'satirical rogue' whom Hamlet reads says, their eyes 'purge
thick amber and plum-tree gum'.[50] Finally they were conquered
by the cold and dry melancholy. Before this coldness and dryness reached too great a height, they became excellent counsellors
and statesmen, but they were also suspicious and ungenerous, as
Timon notes:

> These old Fellowes
> Have their ingratitude in them Hereditary:
> Their blood is cak'd, 'tis cold, it sildome flowes,
> 'Tis lack of kindely warmth, they are not kinde;
> And Nature, as it growes againe toward earth,
> Is fashion'd for the iourney, dull and heavy.[51]

A healthy old age depended on a life of temperance:

> Do we not see many old men, lusty, mery, and wel-complexioned,
> strong of limmes, good footemen, and in their old dayes as fresh and
> active as many yong men be: all which commeth upon no other
> cause, but that in the youthfull dayes, they lived orderly and well,
> and spent not thir adolescencie in unruly riot and lechery,

says Lemnius; we may compare Adam's account of himself in
As You Like It.[52] The characteristics of the different ages fitted in
well with the theory of Decorum, which would have it that

> to worke a Commedie kindly, grave old men should instruct [and]
> yonge men should showe the imperfections of youth . . .[53]

There was again something suspect about uncharacteristic behaviour. In Elizabethan drama there is nearly always a fated quality about very forward children, as there is about Mamilius. Lemnius testifies to this:

> And we observe in all kind of plants and fruits, that those that come late to be ripe, last longest, but those that are soon ripe, are spongy and lither and soon rotten. For ripeness that comes in haste decays first. Wherefore we like in young boys a soon ripe and hasty wit the worst, as also many gifts of nature, or endowments of body or mind, that come on more hastily that ordinarily they use to do, or is fit for that age. For such are found not to be so long lived, and to dye in a short time.[54]

Similarly Falstaff's essential disorderliness is seen in the way he retains many of the qualities of the youthful mind while displaying the physical signs of old age. To the Elizabethans, his frequent inclusion of himself among the young would not only be comic; it would have a slightly sinister note. The Elizabethans preferred people to behave naturally or 'decently'—that is, in the way appropriate to their age, sex, station, profession and so on.

After Heredity, Sex, and Age come what were usually called the 'Six Non-natural Things'. These were: Food, Emptiness and Repletion, Air, Sleep, Exercise and Rest, and the Passions or Perturbations of the Mind. All these altered the condition of the body from the outside, as it were; they were sometimes called 'necessary causes' of the bodily state because they were unavoidable.[55] They were also sometimes spoken of as seven, to correspond with the seven Natural Things, which ultimately depended on them. The Natural Things were the four humours, elements or temperaments, and the three faculties, actions, virtues or spirits—vegetable, vital and animal.[56]

Since the substance of man's body depended on what he ate, diet was of the utmost importance both physiologically and psychologically. The crudest theory was that the eater of the flesh of animals acquired the characteristics of the animals he ate:

> I am a great eater of beefe, and I beleeve that does harme to my wit,

says Sir Andrew.[57] The more 'modern' view was that as food, like everything else, was compounded of the elements, it had a direct effect on the complexion of the body. Huarte explains that concoction cannot completely change the nature of the food eaten:

> we must weet, that albeit a good stomacke do parboile / and alter the meat, and spoile the same of his former quality, yet it doth never utterly deprive it selfe of them: for if we eat lettice (whose qualities is cold and moist) the bloud engendred thereof, shal be cold and moist. . . . And if we eat honny (whose quality is hot & dry) the bloud which we breed, shalbe hot and drie, . . . for it is impossible, (as *Galen* avoucheth) that the humours should not retaine the substances and the qualities, which the meat had, before such time as it was eaten.[58]

There is a combination of both these ideas in the traditional connection of the hare with melancholy. Hare's flesh is cold and dry, and the hare is a solitary, timid creature; it was obvious, therefore, that the meat of the hare would breed the melancholic humour.[59]

The first essential of food was that it should be what Lowe calls 'good aliment'—that is, nourishing and easily digested. As good aliment Lowe cites, *inter alia*, capons, partridges, veal, mutton, yolk of egg, good wine and good and 'well-sodden' ale. Bad aliment included bacon and pork (which was thought to cause leprosy), salt beef, goat's flesh, water fowl, and more surprisingly, cheese, fruit and all sorts of 'legumes'.[60] There was (naturally enough) much disagreement over these questions. It was agreed, however, that diet should be suited first of all to the time of year. In the cold and wet season of Winter, it was advisable to eat hot and dry meat, and drink 'little and good'. In summer, the meat should be cold and humid (in these contexts meat always means any kind of food) and more drink should be taken. Diet should also be suited to age: young children, for example, should eat 'humid meats', which would not dry up their natural moisture and so hinder growth.[61] Most important of all, diet should be designed to correct, rather than to aggravate, natural temperament. A choleric man should avoid fat, salt, or spiced meats, sweet wine, honey or any food of a hot and dry nature. Walkington adds that he should be sparing in his use of tobacco, which dries up the brain.[62] Grumio and Petruchio make the fear that it might aggravate her natural choler the excuse for denying Katherine food.[63] Phlegmatics should avoid cold, damp foods, such as most kinds of fish, water-fowl, salads and heavy, 'corny' ale. Bright and Burton have long sections on the foods to be avoided by melancholiacs. It is easier to say what they admit rather than what they disallow; the general principle they lay down is that melancholiacs should confine themselves to light and easily digested food of a hot, moist nature.[64] Sanguine men were in the happiest position at the table. The main danger for them was that they would eat too much, and particularly over-indulge in red meat and wine, which would put them in danger of breeding too much blood.

Of drinks, ale was only admissible if it was clear, bright and 'well-sodden'. When we remember that at this period stagnant or at any rate impure water was favoured by brewers because it provided a thicker brew, we can only feel that physicians were right in regarding ale with some suspicion. Wine, however, was cordial, as long as it was not too heavy or excessively spiced:

> for it engendreth very pure bloud, it is very quickly converted into nourishment, it helpeth to make digestion in all parts of the body, it giveth courage, purgeth the braine, refresheth the understanding, rejoyceth the heart, quickeneth the spirits. . . .[65]

Falstaff's account of the virtues of sherris-sack, if somewhat rhetorically expressed, is medically sound.[66] Tamburlaine refers to the idea that wine was especially easily concocted into blood:

> Hast thou not seene my horsmen charge the foe,
> Shot through the armes, cut overthwart the hands,
> Dieing their lances with their streaming blood,
> And yet at night carrouse within my tent,
> Filling their empty vaines with aiery wine,
> That being concocted, turnes to crimson blood . . .[67]

Wine, like both air and blood, was hot and moist in quality, and therefore most suitable to the production of both Blood and Vital Spirits, but no doubt the ultimate source for this is to be found in the obvious resemblance between blood and red wine, reinforced by religious symbolism. Excessive drinking, of course, over-heated the blood and caused the brain to be overcome by the fumes arising from the stomach, making 'the receipt of reason / A limbeck only'.[68] The result was first to excite the imagination and relax the control of the reason to the pitch of temporary insanity, and secondly to overcome the spirits entirely so that the drunkard fell into a heavy stupor.

Emptiness and Repletion were obviously connected with Diet. A full stomach drew blood and spirits from the rest of the body to accomplish the process of 'concoction', so that a glutton was naturally stupid, heavy and drowsy. 'Crudity' of the stomach—a term which covered all forms of digestive disorder—not only gave rise to corrupt humours, but distressed the mind in a more direct way:

> For the fulsome vapours (which as it were out of dampishe Marshe or stinkinge Camerine,) strike upward, do annoy the Brayne with greevous / and odious fumes, and distemper the Spirits Animall with a straunge and forreine quality.[69]

It was in this way that indigestion produced nightmares and evil dreams. Melancholy both caused dyspepsia and was caused by it. Ill-digested food bred corrupt humours, which by definition were kinds of melancholy; on the other hand the natural function of the melancholic humour in digestion, which was to assist the retention of the food, led in excess to constipation. This is the origin of 'the melancholy of Moorditch' and the pun in the name Jaques (=Jakes).[70] Any stoppage of the natural excretory processes would give rise to unnatural humours. Most writers give as causes of Melancholy the suppression of the menses in women, the 'staying' of haemorrhoids and 'the intermission of Venus'.[71] A physician called in to a case of mental disorder (or indeed to almost any illness) would inquire first if the patient's recent history included any 'oppilation', and would remedy this before trying any other treatment. A purge of hellebore was the traditional remedy for melancholy, and, of course, the whole practice of phlebotomy was based on the principle that all illness was caused by the presence of excess or corrupt humour in the blood:

> which is the cause that often in the cure of these affects, the Phisitians are necessarily busied in tempering the Blood, that is, bringing to a mediocrity the 4 humors composing the masse of blood, if they at any time offend in quantity or quality. For whether if any thing abound, or digresse from the wonted temper in any excesse of heat, cold, viscosity, grosseness, thinnes, or any such like quality, none of

the accustomed functions will be well performed. For which cause
those chiefe helpes to preserve and restore health have been divinely
invented; *Phelebotomy*, or bloodletting, which amends the qualities
of too much blood; and purging which corrects and draws away the
viscous quality.[72]

Starvation and excessive purging naturally weakened the body,
and over-indulgence in sexual intercourse was as much a cause
of Melancholy as unnatural abstention.[73] A sufficiency of good
and digestible food would obviously put the body in 'a good
humour', as Menenius considers when he is asked to undertake
an embassy to Coriolanus:

> Ile undertak't:
> I thinke hee'l heare me. Yet to bite his lip,
> And humme at good *Cominius*, much unhearts mee.
> He was not taken well, he had not din'd,
> The Veines unfill'd, our blood is cold, and then
> We powt upon the Morning, are unapt
> To give or to forgive; but when we have stufft
> These Pipes, and these Conveyances of our blood
> With Wine and Feeding, we have suppler Soules
> Then in our Priest-like Fasts: therefore Ile watch him
> Till he be dieted to my request,
> And then Ile set upon him.[74]

The quality of the air was important because it entered into
the composition of the spirits. The most desirable was pure,
fresh, clear and 'subtle' upland air. Mountain air was too thin
and cold; lowland air too still, damp and heavy. Fenny or marshy
air was injurious to the health, and bred melancholy.[75] Air that
had been well warmed by the 'genial heat' of the sun was most
healthy. Night air was obnoxious, as Portia says:

> Is *Brutus* sicke? And is it Physicall
> To walke unbraced, and sucke up the humours
> Of the danke Morning? What, is Brutus sicke?
> And will he steale out of his wholsome bed
> To dare the vile contagion of the Night?
> And tempt the Rhewmy, and unpurged Ayre,
> To adde unto his sicknesse?[76]

Different winds had different effects on the body. On the whole
winds from the North and East were regarded as healthy; those

from the South and West as unhealthy. There was much disagreement about this, but the damp South wind was nearly
always regarded as bad. Lemnius says it causes gout, rheumatism,
apoplexy, miscarriage of pregnant women, and whooping-
cough in children.[77] There was probably a connection with the
idea of southern countries as the home of diseases—not least the
'Neapolitan evil'.[78] High winds and cloudy or stormy weather
were recognized as having a depressing effect on the health and
spirits; a calm, clear sky allowed the sun to exercise its beneficent
influence.[79]

The temperature of the air depended on Climate, which
played a considerable part in shaping the characters of men.
Some held that a man's internal temperature was opposite to the
climate in which he lived, those living in hot climates having
cold natures and so on, but the more straightforward view was
the most common. Thus Southerners were of a hot temperament; they were quick, subtle, ingenious and witty—

> For never yet was *foole* a *Florentine*
> (As by the wise hath well observed byn)
> So subtill is the Aire he draweth in—[80]

but also proud, arrogant, suspicious, jealous and revengeful.
Lemnius says of Italians that they

> will beare in memorie a long time things past, and will not lightly
> suffer any grudge to grow out of remembraunce. And if any wronge
> bee done unto them, they will revyve the memory thereof after
> many yeares. . . . Which affection I do ascribe unto heate, which doth
> so exceedingly exulcerate and distemper their mynds with indigna-
> tion, that, humour and moystnes, is not able to alay, quench and
> qualefye it.[81]

This answers well to the portrayal of Italians in Elizabethan and
Jacobean drama. Those living even further South were of a still
more violent nature. Lowe says:

> The people towards the South are melancholick, cruel vindicatyf,
> always timide, they are subject to be madde and furious, as often
> chanceth in the Realme of *Feze* and *Marock,* in *Africa, Ethiopia* and
> *Egypt,* where there is a great number of mad men.[82]

Neither the wickedness of Aaron nor the fury of Othello would
therefore come as a surprise to the Elizabethan psychologist.

Northerly people were steadier of temperament, stronger and
more beautiful, but they were also more stupid:

> The Northern *Nations* are more moist, and cold,
> Lesse wicked and deceiptfull, faithfull, just,
> More ample, strong, couragious, martiall, bold,
> And, for their bloud is colder, lesse they lust:
> Then cold bloud being thick, it follow must
> They are less witty, and more barberous;
> And for they inwardly are more adust,
> They *meate* and *drinke* devour as ravenous,
> The *paunch* and *pot* esteeming precious.[83]

In saying that these nations are 'inwardly more adust' (or hot)
Davies is following the view that inner temperature is opposed
to outward climate. The characteristics he gives were in any
case generally accepted.

English and French writers are usually careful to point out
that their own nations lie between the two extremes, and par-
take of the virtues of both and the defects of neither. The English
suspected the French of most of the Italian vices, while admiring
their cleverness and culture. The French view of the English is
expressed by the Constable in *Henry V*:

> *Dieu de Battailes*, where have they this mettell?
> Is not their Clymate foggy, raw, and dull?
> On whom, as in despight, the Sunne lookes pale,
> Killing their Fruit with frownes. Can sodden Water,
> A Drench for sur-reyn'd Jades, their Barly broth,
> Decoct their cold blood to such valiant heat?
> And shall our quick blood, spirited with Wine,
> Seeme frostie?[84]

This speech combines the effect on character of Climate and Diet.
Lemnius, who as a Dutchman may be regarded as an independent witness, says that the English are comely, well-proportioned
and 'well-complexioned'. They are not naturally good scholars
or artists, but if they are led to study they persist until they
become learned. In disposition they are proud, easily angered
and revengeful. The French are eloquent, ingenious, lively,
lusty, 'dapper', and nimble. If they are not well disciplined they
are inconstant, captious, deceitful, false-hearted, and enamoured
of change. They are also 'babblative and full of much vaine

talking'.[85] The English would probably not have quarrelled
much with Lemnius' views.

Exercise, rest and sleep fall naturally under consideration
together. Lemnius is firm in his praise of exercise:

> Nothing is holesomer nor more avayleable for health, then season-
> able Exercyse and convenient motion. For by it the quicknes and
> vigour of the mynde is revyved, the faynt drowsye Spyrites styrred
> up and awaked, the soule and mynde cheered and exhilarated, all the
> parts of the body and all the senses both within and without made
> nimble, active, perfect and ready to do their proper functions: the
> colour fayrer and fresher, the appetite provoked and sharpened . . .
> excrements commodiously purged, concoction speedelyer finished
> and the juyce or humours (being well concocted) better distributed
> to the sustenaunce and nourishment of every member of the body.[86]

Idleness sowed the seeds of mental and physical illness in the
body as weeds grew in untilled ground; Burton regards it as one
of the chief sources of melancholy.[87] As always, the principle of
the Golden Mean had to be borne in mind. Too much exercise
of body and mind wasted the spirits and dulled the faculties, as
Berowne says:

> Why, universall plodding poysons up
> The nimble spirits in the arteries,
> As motion and long during action tyres
> The sinnowy vigour of the travailer.[88]

Labourers and 'clowns' were thus dull-witted and slow, and
statesmen and scholars, who exercised their brains beyond
moderation, were subject to melancholy and debility. Sleep was
essential to health. Langton sums up its virtues:

> And thys same rest is good for .iii. causes, fyrst to moysten the
> brayne, and then to the generation of spirits, and laste of all, to make
> an end of concoction in the stomake and liver.[89]

The body and brain being at rest, and the senses dormant, the
animal spirits were quiescent, and the vegetable and vital spirits
were able to apply themselves to restoring the tissues, while

> native heate gathering it self inward, is of more force / and strongly
> applyeth concoction, perfourming the same not onely in the Stom-
> ack, but also through the whole bodye besyde, whose vapour and
> plesaunt sent moysteneth the brayne and bringeth asleep the Instru-
> ments of the Senses.[90]

Sleep's function of allowing the final concoction of food, whereby it became completely assimilated by the body, justifies Macbeth's description of it as

> great Natures second Course,
> Chiefe nourisher in Life's Feast . . .[91]

It is part of Lear's tragedy that he is not allowed to recover his faculties in sleep, as Kent realizes:

> Oppress'd nature sleepes,
> This rest might yet have balmed thy broken sinewes,
> Which if convenience will not alow,
> Stand in hard cure.[92]

The effect of the Passions and Perturbations on the body must be left till later. To the causes of temperament so far listed Burton adds what he calls 'Supernatural Causes'—God, Angels, Devils, Spirits and Stars.[93] Of God it is hardly necessary to speak, since he was creator of all life and shaper of every man's destiny. The influence of Angels (and the debate whether each man had or had not a Guardian Angel) was the province of the theologian. 'Spirits' or 'intelligences', good or evil, were similarly the concern of necromancers and hermetic philosophers rather than physicians and psychologists. The power of Devils was, however, still of serious concern. Some writers maintained that God permitted the Devil, once he had succeeded in tempting the Soul to sin, actually to interfere in the operations of body and Soul, but this view was much combated. The belief that he could insinuate himself into the body of man—as in *Paradise Lost* he does into the body of the serpent—was losing ground by 1600. It might be, however, that devils might affect the body (and therefore the Soul) by means of the non-natural things:

> the evil spirits mingle themselves with our food, humours, spirits, with the ayre and breath, that we draw in and breathe out, and they pollute many other things that serve for our use, and whereby our health is preserved.[94]

A still more 'rational' explanation was that the Devil and his minions took advantage of an already existing disposition of the body to tempt the soul:

> Thus, do they incite and egge those that abound with Bloud, and be sanguine complexioned, to riot, wantonesse, drunkennesse, wastful-

nes, prodigality, filthy and detestable loves, horrible lusts, incest and
buggerie. . . . Them that be Melancholique, unto envy, emulation,
bitternesse, hatred, spite, sorcery, fraude, subtlety, deceipte, treason,
sorrow, heavinesse, desperation, distrust, and last of all to a lament-
able and shamefull end.[95]

Hamlet is thns quite justified in thinking that the Devil

> perhaps
> Out of my Weaknesse, and my Melancholly,
> As he is very potent with such Spirits,
> Abuses me to damne me.[96]

In a similar fashion it was possible to explain away the supernatural powers claimed by witches and warlocks by saying that
the Devil merely deceived them into thinking that they performed wonders when in fact they did not. Reginald Scot in
England (like Weyer on the Continent) went even further in
suggesting that many witches were feeble-minded from old age
or suffering from some kind of hysteria, and that their devilish
powers were in fact hallucinatory:

> if anie man advisedlie marke their words, actions, cogitations, and
> gestures, he shall perceive that melancholie abounding in their head,
> and occupieng their braine, hath deprived or rather depraved their
> judgements, and all their senses: I meane not of coosening witches,
> but of poore melancholike women, which are themselves de-
> ceived . . .[97]

The movement towards a rational explanation of the apparently
supernatural is well illustrated in the title of Edward Jorden's
pamphlet on uterine hysteria:

> A Brief Discourse of a Disease called the Suffocation of the Mother.
> Written upon occasion which hath of late been taken thereby, to
> suspect possession of an evill spirit, or some such-like supernaturall
> power. Wherein it is declared that divers strange actions and passions
> of the body of man, which in the common opinion, are imputed to
> the Divell, have their true naturall cause, and do accompanie this
> disease.

All these matters were, however, in dispute. Weyer was answered
by Bodin, and Scot's *Discoverie of Witchcraft* provoked a number
of replies, of which the most famous is King James' *Demonologie*.
Witchcraft and possession were more the concern of the theo-

logian and the canon lawyer than the physician or psychologist.
Medical men were not in agreement: Lemnius, for example,
denies the possibility of possession, but Paré affirms it.[98] In
Jacobean England, with a demonologist on the throne, it was not
profitable to profess open scepticism. The dramatists, at all
events, and among them Shakespeare, seem not to doubt the
reality of witchcraft, and everyone was agreed that in some way
or other the Devil had power to influence the minds of men.

The influence of the Stars on the body and mind of man was
a subject of formidable complexity. The 'science' of Astrology
came to England fairly late, and it never had quite the same
grasp over men's minds here that it had on the Continent. In
Elizabethan and Jacobean times it was quite customary for
nativities to be cast at the birth of a child, and for an astrologer
to be consulted whenever any decisive step had to be taken. It
is difficult to see what proportion real belief, superstition, and
mere fashion played in the current attitude to Astrology. The
astrologers, like the alchemists, were to a certain extent protected
from attacks by the very complexity of their art. If their pro-
phecies were unfulfilled they could always point to the number
of factors which they had to take into account, the overlooking
of any one of which might vitiate their calculations. They had
also the excuse that no two of their authorities ever agreed completely—a fact which does not render an account of their beliefs
any easier. The dramatists are nearly always content with quite
general references to the influence of the stars; they display none
of the detailed knowledge of the subject which Chaucer deployed.
As with Demonology, there was a wide range of views about
astrology. At one extreme was flat unbelief, which Cassius
voices, and Edmund:

> This is the excellent foppery of the world, that when we are sicke in
> fortune, often the surfets of our own behaviour, we make guilty of
> our disasters, the Sun, the Moone, and Starres, as if we were villains
> on necessitie, Fooles by heavenly compulsion, Knaves, Theeves, and
> Treachers by Sphericall predominance. Drunkards, Lyars and Adul-
> terers by an inforc'd obedience of Planatary influence, and all that
> we are evill in, by a divine thrusting on . . .[99]

The fact that this is put into Edmund's mouth would tend to
suggest that Shakespeare himself was not in sympathy with

these views, though we cannot reach certainty here. Shakespeare
perhaps subscribed rather to the view which Gloucester expresses
immediately before this speech of Edmund's—that the stars,
although they do not cause events on earth, are signs that such
events are about to take place:

> These late Eclipses in the Sun and Moone portend no good to us:
> though the wisedome of Nature can reason it thus, and thus, yet
> Nature finds it selfe scourg'd by the sequent effects.[100]

The ultimate ground for this belief was the unity of the Universe, and the relation between the microcosm and the macro-
cosm. The essential unity of the Universe was also called into
account by those who wished to maintain the absolute domination of 'the Heavens' over the life of men: it was impossible—
so ran the argument—that the movements of such large and
powerful bodies should not affect all else in the frame of Nature.
To this could be added a belief in 'influence', the actual quasi-
material radiation by which the stars and planets transmitted
their 'virtue' to men and beasts, and even to plants and stones.
(We retain a trace of this in the name 'influenza'.) There was
also to be adduced the identity between the substance of the
soul and the quintessence of which all translunary things were
formed. The view based on these arguments—that directly
opposed to Edmund's scepticism—was too fatalistic ever to be
acceptable to Christianity.

The most usual view is a compromise. It was admitted that
the stars might tend to make a man of a certain disposition, or
incline him to a particular course of action. They might do this
for the reasons already mentioned, or it might be that they could
affect the atmosphere, and so men's bodies, and ultimately their
minds. Comets and meteors, for example, might dry up the air,
so that men became choleric, and wars and rebellions ensued.
Their power here, however, was only of the same order as that
of the non-natural things, and above all they could not affect
the freedom of the will:

> And yet not that their power performeth entire effects. For with
> them (as we have heard) concurre the diet, manners, nativitie, and
> place, but above all the liberty of the minde is alwaies dominant, to
> moderate and governe all the inclinations thereof . . .[101]

The tag always quoted in this context is *sapiens dominabitur astris*: the wise man will govern the stars.

This position granted, it became possible to recognize certain types of mind and body as characteristic of men born under different signs and planets, with the (sometimes tacit) proviso that these influences could be withstood and overcome. We should have little difficulty in recognizing some at least of the planetary types. The 'Jovial' man, for example, was handsome, bold, just, generous, cheerful, and open-hearted. Batman says that

> in man's body [Jupiter] helpeth to fairenesse and honestie; for he giveth white colour, and faire, medled with redness; and giveth faire eyen and teethe, and faire haire, faire beard and round.[102]

In this Jupiter's association with the qualities of Air and the sanguine complexion are apparent. Mars, as we might expect,

> hath mastrie over cholar, fire, and cholaricke complection, and disposeth to boldnesse and hardinesse, and to desire of wreake.

Because of his heat, Mars made men tall and thin, and in later life stooping and crooked. He disposed men to be smiths or bakers, or to engage in any craft involving the use of fire. The Saturnine disposition might incline men to prudence and learning, but Saturn, like Mars, had an evil as well as a good aspect. In his evil aspect Mars made men furious, violent, wrathful and rebellious: the cold and dry Saturn was even more liable to produce ill effects. He made men foul of body, slow and heavy of movement, miserable in mind, and subject to melancholy. Saturnians were often miserly, deceitful, revengeful, fraudulent, treacherous and envious. Those born under Venus were fair, graceful, amiable and voluptuous. To this plant belonged singers, lovers of music,

> makers of confections of spicerie and spicers, goldsmithes, and taylours to shape womens cloathing.

Venus, naturally, was more suitable to dominate in a woman's than a man's nativity. Mercury, the god of Wisdom and Eloquence, made men subtle, shrewd, loquacious and cunning; he was the patron of merchants and thieves, as well as of orators and men of learning and science. The Sun was a beneficent planet: according to Batman (quoting Ptolemy) it maketh a man corpulent, great of body, faire of face, and well coloured, with great eyen, and maketh a man able to all works of gold.

Fludd says it makes men prudent, eloquent, sober, fair, truthful and religious.[103] 'Sunny' appears to have been applied first to appearance, in the sense 'handsome, cheerful', and afterwards to disposition. The moon was a planet of great importance in the casting of horoscopes and also in astrological medicine. In the first place the effect of the other planets depended on their relation to her, and in the second, her moist, watery nature gave her especial affinity to the brain and the marrow of the backbone, and to the humours. She governed the humours, in fact, in the same way as she governed the tides:

> The Moone increaseth all humours: for by privye passings of kinde, floude / and ebbe is increased and multiplyed. In hir waning the marrow of the bones, the braine of the head, and humours of the body be made lesse: and in wexing and incresing of hir, they are increased, and therfore all thing hath compassion of the default of the Moone.[104]

It is not surprising, therefore, to learn that 'The Moone maketh a man unstable'. 'Lunatic' soon acquired the sense of 'inconstant', 'subject to unpredictable changes of mood' and thus shaded off into our modern meaning:

> It is the very error of the Moone,
> She comes more neerer Earth then she was wont,
> And makes men mad.[105]

The effect of the signs of the Zodiac was connected with the domination each had over a particular part of the body. Taurus, for example, governed the neck and throat—not 'sides and heart' as Sir Andrew thinks, nor 'legs and thighs' as Sir Toby says.[106] Consequently this sign gave a man a large face, a crooked, heavy nose with large nostrils, heavy eyes, stiff black hair, and, as we might expect, a 'bullneck'. It also made him shamefast and honest, but vain and idle. Cancer

> hath mastery in the body over the brest, ribbes and lungs: and maketh greatness in the bodye. For from the middle he maketh a man great and of evill shape, and boistous, and upward subtill, and maketh short teeth and crooked.

Leo, which governed the stomach, brawnes, heart and back, made men 'great upward and small beneath', and, of course, brave and 'lion-hearted'.[107] There is a curious mixture in all this of a somewhat arbitrary division of responsibility with an attempt to attribute qualities appropriate to the animals after which some of the signs are named. There is, moreover, considerable disagreement among the authorities. The finer points, together with the very intricate problems of the casting of horoscopes, are only relevant to the study of astrology proper, and not to the study of psychological theory.[108]

The general attitude to all these factors which could affect the condition of the body and so of the mind was the same as the attitude to the influence of the stars. It would be not only foolish but impious to deny that Age, Heredity, Climate, Diet and so on had an inescapable effect on Man. To deny this would be to set up Man as a creature independent of the world about him, and so independent of God. On the other hand, it would be equally irreligious to assume that any or all of these things had absolute power over the Soul, which would entail the assumption that Man had no control over his destiny. The correct attitude was to admit that these things had a power which was inescapable, and might in a weak man be decisive, but that the wise man could control and mitigate their effects. Such a man would learn his own nature, avoid any aggravation of whatever dangerous tendencies he suspected in himself, and use every means to reduce himself to the ideal of the Golden Mean. Lear's tragedy comes about because 'he hath ever but slenderly known himself',[109] and has taken no steps to check his natural choler, or to avoid occasions which will increase it. 'Nosce Teipsum' was not an idle catch-phrase, but a vital rule of conduct.

Chapter Four

THE BODY'S EFFECT ON THE SOUL

THE theory of the structure of body and soul which has been outlined could claim to provide a fairly satisfactory explanation of most of the immediately observable mental and physical phenomena. The theory also satisfactorily discharged what from some points of view was its primary function —that of explaining how sin and disorder could apparently be present in the perfect and incorruptible soul. Blame for all failures of the mind could be laid on the body, or on external conditions affecting the body. Some writers, it is true, attempted to maintain the Platonic view that it was the Soul's duty to maintain health in the body, and that disease was the outward sign of an inward corruption. Absolutely maintained, however, this view was unacceptable to the theologian, and it was usual to admit only that disorder in the soul must have some effect on the body. Many categorically denied that any defect at all was possible, at least in the rational soul. The usual view was that the body was at best a prison to the soul, even if it was not her natural enemy. Tamyra, after yielding to Bussy, thus sums up the position:

> Our bodies are but thick clouds to our souls,
> Through which they cannot shine when they desire . . .[1]

No mind could reveal itself truly in a sickly body, as Lear reminds himself when he is trying to account for the behaviour of Cornwall:

> No, but not yet, may be he is not well,
> Infirmity doth still neglect all office,
> Whereto our health is bound, we are not our selves,
> When Nature being opprest, commands the mind
> To suffer with the body . . .[2]

Even in a man who was not actually ill the nature and condition of the body would affect the disposition and the mind.

The exact composition of the body in terms of the elements was of primary importance. Man's life, as Sir Toby correctly says, consists of the four elements, as does everything else in the created universe:

> therefore, boldly it is to be professed, that Fire, Water, Ayre and Earthe, to be the first, and the common, and most simple Elementes, and beginners of all things, of which verily, both Plantes, and also all living creatures, are engendered, nourished and encreased . . .[3]

A perfectly balanced mixture of the elements would be immortal and incorruptible: 'whatever dies was not mixed equally.'[4] Indeed, some believed that the soul, like the stars, was composed of the fifth element or quintessence, which was a perfect mixture of the other four, and therefore changeless and timeless.[5] This view, however, was not universally accepted. Some again said that the soul was of a fiery nature, but this was more of a metaphor than a statement of fact.[6] Simple correspondences could be found between the elements and the parts of Man: for example, between the body and earth, the humours and water, blood and air, and the spirits and fire.[7] It was plain that at death the lighter elements would ascend to Heaven through natural appetite, while the heavier elements returned to earth, to which they were akin.

> I am Fire, and Ayre, my other Elements
> I give to baser Life,

says Cleopatra,[8] emphasizing her courage and her joyful determination as well as her feeling that she has sloughed off her body and is already all soul. In general terms, Fire and Air were usually associated with vitality and happiness: Water and Earth with death and sorrow. Thus the academic play *Pathomachia* speaks of:

> Hope, which like Fire, is hot and drie: Joy like Aire moyst and warme: Griefe like water cold and moyst. And Feare like Earth dry and cold.[9]

Shakespeare makes extended use of this symbolism in sonnets XLIV and XLV: in *Henry V*, the Dauphin celebrates the speed, action and courage of his horse in elemental terms:

> It is a Beast for *Perseus*: hee is pure Ayre and Fire; and the dull Elements of Earth and Water never appeare in him, but only in

patient stillnesse while his Rider mounts him: hee is indeede a Horse, and all other Jades you may call Beasts.[10]

There can be no doubt that Ariel and Caliban are elemental creatures in a strict sense: Ariel's name itself suggests a nature composed of air and fire, and Caliban's character suggests a mixture of the heavy, dull, and intractable elements of earth and water.

The mixture of elements in man produced psychological effects which could be analysed in much more detail. There was debate whether it was preferable to examine character in terms of the humours or in terms of the elements, but as each humour corresponded to an element it made little practical difference which method was followed. A more real distinction was between men in whom one of the four primary qualities predominated, and those in whom a blend of two qualities was dominant. Lemnius deals with all the possible combinations, and is therefore a suitable guide to follow, although his method involves some repetition. He begins by stating categorically:

> All the Complexion and temperament of mans bodye proceedeth from the powers of the Elementes, and not of the Humours; and of them is the whole body tempered and compounded.[11]

He then lists first the complexion 'perfectly and exactly temperate' which is 'the pattern of virtue'.[12] The perfect balance of elements would of course imply balance of the qualities and of the humours as well. This ideal state was not found on earth, or only very rarely, but it might be imagined as a norm against which to measure other 'temperatures'. Physically men of a perfect complexion would be tall, well proportioned, fair of face, and with a sweet, gentle and noble expression. Their hair would be of a golden or auburn colour, long and gently waving, and their eyes blue or bluish-grey. Their gait would be majestical, their glance commanding, their voice harmonious and their whole presence gracious and impressive. In everything but stature, the little freckled knight who fights in the tournament in *The Two Noble Kinsmen* seems to be such a man:

> He's white hair'd,
> Not wanton white, but such a manly colour
> Next to an aborne; tough, and nimble set,
> Which showes an active soule; his arms are brawny,

> Linde with strong sinewes: To the shoulder peece
> Gently they swell, like women new conceav'd,
> Which speakes him prone to labour, never fainting
> Under the waight of Armes: stout-hearted, still,
> But when he stirs, a Tiger; he's gray eyd,
> Which yeelds compassion where he conquers: sharpe
> To spy advantages, and where he finds 'em,
> He's swift to make 'em his: He do's no wrongs,
> Nor takes none; he's round fac'd, and when he smiles
> He showes a Lover, when he frownes, a Souldier. . . .[13]

In character such men were grave, noble, gentle, generous, amiable, courageous, self-controlled—in fact, a compound of all the virtues. Brutus is so described:

> This was the Noblest Roman of them all:
> All the Conspirators save only hee,
> Did what they did, in envy of great Caesar:
> He, onely in a generall honest thought,
> And common good to all, made one of them.
> His life was gentle, and the Elements
> So mixt in him, that Nature might stand up,
> And say to all the world; This was a man.[14]

Crites in *Cynthia's Revels* is similarly characterized:

> A creature of a most perfect and divine temper. One, in whom the humours and elements are peaceably met, without emulation of precedencie: he is neyther too phantastikely melancholy, too slowly phlegmaticke, too lightly sanguine, or too rashly cholericke, but in all, so composde & ordr'd, as it is cleare, *Nature* went about some ful worke, she did more then make a man, when she made him . . .[15]

The false Scroope appeared, but was not, of this happy type.[16] This temperament had, in its command of passion and its indifference to the blows of Fortune, points of contact with the Stoic or 'Senecall Man', as for example he is portrayed by Chapman in Clermont D'Ambois, but in fact it did not preclude the experience and indeed the expression of 'manly' emotion. As always, the key-note was temperance, rather than repression; sobriety and reasoned faith, rather than the self-sufficiency of rationalism.

Besides the perfect temperament, Lemnius lists eight 'intemperatures'. The first four of these are 'simple intemperatures'

produced by a preponderance of one of the four primary qualities. In such cases one quality dominates over its opposite, and
the remaining two are in equipoise. In the man of hot 'temperature', for example, the qualities of moisture and dryness balance
each other. The characteristics of the four simple intemperatures
may be briefly set down. Men of a hot temperature were lean
of body; their skins were of a reddish, or in hotter countries
brownish, colour. The hair of their head was darker than their
beard, and was usually black and curled or 'crooked' like a
negro's. (This was because the 'third excrement' which formed
the hair became parched and shrivelled in its passage through
their hot brain.) Men of this temperature were of a warlike,
proud, rash, and lecherous nature. Men of a cold temperature
were unhealthy, since cold was the quality most inimical to vital
heat. They had a hairless, smooth, cold skin, and their flesh was
flabby and of a dead-white or leaden colour. Their voices were
low, faltering and feminine, and they were stupid and cowardly.
The dry temperament was little better, since moisture was also
vital to life. The skin of men of this nature was 'scurvy, rugged
and unseemly', and of a swart or yellow colour. This temperament made them also 'grim-visaged' and 'filthy, loathsome and
leane as a rake'. Their voices were feeble and slight, their pulse
faint, their gait slow, their eyes hollow, their hair scanty, their
lips pale, their temples shrunken, their cheeks 'hanging', their
nails crooked, and their ears cold and 'crumpled'. Their memories were bad, they slept little, and their state in general was low.
Scholars were particularly liable to fall into this condition
through overmuch study and lack of exercise. The moist temperature, on the other hand, was not so unfavourable, unless
moisture overcame vital heat. In this temperature the body was
soft, white-skinned, smooth, and hairless. The hair was straight
and thick, and pale in colour; the eyes grey or blue, bright and
protuberant. The expression was usually cheerful. Men of this
nature were low in stature and tended towards corpulence;
their minds were rather dull; they were of faint courage and
little given to lechery.[17]

Of greater importance, from a more strictly psychological
point of view, was the effect of the qualities on the mental faculties proper. Here arose a great difficulty, which Charron points
out:

Temperature is the mixture and proportion of the foure first qualities
... and it may be a fift besides, which is the Harmonie of these foure.
Now from the Temperature of the braine proceedeth all the state
and action of the reasonable *Soule*, but that which is the cause of
great misery unto man, is, that the three faculties of the reasonable
Soule ... do require and exercise themselves by contrarie temperatures.

He goes on to note that the Understanding required for its
proper working a dry temperature in the brain,

> whereby it comes to pass that they that are striken in yeeres, do excell
> those in their understanding that are yoong, because in the braine as
> yeeres increese, so moisture decreaseth. So likewise melancholicke
> men, such as are afflicted with want, and fast much (for heaviness
> and fasting are driers) are wise and ingenious, *Splendor siccus, animus
> sapientissimus, velatio dat intellectum* ...

The temperature most suitable to memory was moist, with a
kind of oily moisture apt to receive impressions:

> whereof it is that infants have better memorie than old men, and the
> morning after that humidity that is gotten by sleepe in the night, is
> more apt for memorie, which is likewise more vigorous in Northerne
> people ...[18]

Other writers prefer a dry temperature for memory, for although it takes impressions less easily, it retains them longer. The
process of memorizing seems always to be thought of as a storing
of mental images, usually compared to the imprint of a seal on
wax.[19] Most authorities agree that the memory of old men, such
as Polonius, is bad; Spenser follows poetic convention rather than
psychological theory in making the Recorder of the House of
Alma an old man. It was generally accepted that Heat was the
quality best suited to the Imagination:

> from whence it commeth that franticke men, and such as are sicke of
> burning maladies, are excellent in that that belongs to the imagina-
> tion, as *Poetry, Divination*, and that it hath greatest force in yoong
> men, and of middle yeares (Poets and Prophets have / flourished in
> this age) and in the middle parts betwixt North and South.

The cold quality was of no value to the faculties of the mind.[20]
   As Charron points out, the difficulty was that the three active
qualities could hardly exist together, or not at least to any

marked degree. It was almost impossible, for example, to possess an excellent memory and a vivid imagination, for these two faculties demanded opposed qualities. The hot temperature of madmen over-stimulated their imagination, but made their memory uncertain, and therefore Hamlet offers to rebut his mother's suspicion of his sanity by recapitulating what he has said:

> bring me to the Test
> And I the matter will re-word: which madnesse
> Would gamboll from.[21]

In moderation, however, these qualities could exist together, and indeed it might be desirable that they should act as a check on each other.

After the four simple intemperatures in Lemnius' classification come the four 'compound intemperatures', in which two qualities predominate. These are in fact the same as the four 'temperaments' or 'complexions' in which one element or humour dominates over the rest, since each element or humour possessed two primary qualities. In practice it was most common to attribute the characteristics of these compound intemperature to the effects of the humours, so much so that in common parlance they were most frequently referred to as the 'four humours'. In order to understand more fully the effects of the humours, it is first necessary to look more closely at the physical operation of the passions. Wright provides a conveniently clear summary of the process. The first stage was the perception and the recognition of the object, and the transmission of this information to the heart:

> First then, to our imagination commeth, by sense or memorie, some object to be knowne, convenient or disconvenient to Nature, the which being known . . . in the imagination . . . presently the purer spirits flocke from the brayne, by certayne secret channels to the heart, where they pitch at the doore, signifying what an object was presented, convenient or disconvenient for it . . .

The heart, the seat of the Passions, was responsible for bringing about the physical changes required by the nature of the object:

> The heart immediately bendeth, either to prosecute it or to eschew it; and the better to effect that affection, draweth other humours to help him, and so in pleasure concurre great store of pure spirits; in

payne and sadness much melancholy blood; in ire, blood and choller . . .[22]

This process might be affected at every stage by the physical condition of the body. If, for example, the Animal spirits were weak or feeble, it might not be possible for reports from the sense-organs to reach the Imagination, or for the message of the Imagination to reach the heart, or for the heart to summon the forces necessary to take the requisite action. The two vital centres were obviously the brain and the heart, and both these organs were easily affected by a 'distemperature' of the humours. If the brain were 'distemperatured' the perceptive power would be disordered; either objects would be incorrectly perceived, or the Imagination might persuade the Judgement of the existence of an object which was in fact not present at all. In either case the heart would be called on to provide the physical basis for an inappropriate passion. Such a distemperature of the brain might be caused by a general distemperature of the body, or by a humour which 'settled' in the brain, leaving the rest of the body unaffected. Primaudaye describes a third way in which the humours might affect the brain:

> there is yet another meane whereby these humors, especially the flegmaticke humor, which is of the nature of the water, ascend up unto the braine by reason of vapours arising upward out of the stomack, like to the vapour of a pot seething on the fire with liquor in it, and like vapours that ascend up from the earth into the aire, of which raine is engendred.[23]

This ascension of the humours from the stomach to the brain in the form of 'vapours' or 'fumes' was particularly likely to occur when the stomach was disordered by 'crudities'. Indigestion might thus cause hallucinations, or fits of motiveless passion. Nightmares were the result of this process, and also what Walkington calls 'dreams of complexion'. Thus choleric men dreamed of fireworks, exhalations, comets, meteors, skirmishing and stabbing; sanguine men of beautiful women, of blood and purple colours; phlegmatics of floods, of swimming in rivers, of torrents and sudden showers of rain; melancholiacs of falling down from high towers, of 'travailling in darke and solemne places', of caves, of the Devil and of 'blacke and furious beastes'.[24]

The heart was still more easily affected by the humours. If an excess of humour was present in the body, then the passion called forth would be more fierce than the nature of the object warranted. An excess of melancholy, for example, would cause a man to feel extravagant grief on a trivial occasion. It would also, of course, make it very difficult for him to be moved to the passion of mirth. A deficiency of a humour would also cause difficulty, for the heart would be unable to call up the forces necessary to enable the body to prosecute the necessary action. Hamlet seems to fear this of himself:

> it cannot be
> But I am Pigeon-livr'd, and lack Gall
> To make Oppression bitter.[25]

The constitution of the heart might also be of importance. According to the proportion of the elements in it, the heart could be literally soft or hard, cold or hot. Qualities were sometimes assigned to the passions, and the heart would obviously tend to experience easily those passions similar in quality to itself. Thus Joy, a hot and moist passion, was most natural to those whose hearts were hot and moist, such as children. The cold and dry Fear was appropriate to those of a cold and dry constitution, such as melancholiacs and old people. A soft heart was quickly moved by grief or pity, which a hard heart would experience only with difficulty; a hot heart would be easily moved to anger.[26]

A gross excess of humour would affect both the brain and the heart, with correspondingly more serious effects:

> if both partes be overcharged of humour, the apprehension and affection both are corrupted, and misse of their right action, and so all things mistaken, ingender that confused spirite, and those stormes of outragious love, hatred, hope or feare, wherewith bodies so passionate are heere and there, tossed with disquiet.[27]

The soul then became the prey of what Lemnius calls 'secondary passions'[28]—that is, passions which have no reasonable objective cause. An extremely choleric man, for example, would not only fly into violent rages over trivial matters, but would imagine causes of offence where none existed in reality.

All men were subject to these false passions, to a greater or lesser degree, as Wright says:

And for this cause we may resolve another difficulty, why some men are alwayes, almost, merry; others, for the most part, melancholy; others, ever angry; this diversity must come from the naturall constitution of the body, wherein, one or other humour doth predominate. The selfsame cause may be alledged, why sometimes wee feele ourselves, we know not why, mooved to Mirth, Melancholy, or Anger; insomuch that any little occasion were sufficient to incense that Passion; for, as these humors depend upon the heavens, ayre, sleepe and waking, meate and drinke, exercise and rest; according to the alterations of these externall causes, one or other Humor doth more or lesse overrule the body, and so causeth alteration of the Passions.[29]

It was because the passions thus depended ultimately on the non-natural things that the life of temperance was the ideal: 'for', says Lemnius,

they that are of good bodily temper, and lead a temperate life, and sober diet, are lesse wont to be troubled with passions.[30]

The excess of one or other humour was not in moderation actually dangerous, although it was always potentially so, since the occurrence of suitable circumstances might aggravate the effects of disposition. A gross excess could not but lead to violent passions, and violent passions would lead in turn to sin and damnation. In this way an apparently trivial physical condition might lead to the ruin of an otherwise noble nature, and the destruction of a soul. This is the thought underlying Hamlet's famous speech:

> So oft it chaunces in particuler men,
> That for some vicious mole of nature in them
> As in their birth wherein they are not guilty,
> (Since nature cannot choose his origin)
> By the ore-growth of some complexion
> Oft breaking downe the pales and forts of reason,
> Or by some habit, that too much ore-leavens
> The forme of plausive manners, that these men
> Carrying I say the stamp of one defect
> Being Natures livery, or Fortunes starre,
> His vertues els be they as pure as grace,
> As infinite as man may undergoe,
> Shall in the generall censure take corruption

From that particuler fault: the dram of evile
Doth all the noble substance often dout
To his owne scandle.[31]

The much-disputed 'dram of evile' might be interpreted by a
contemporary psychologist as a 'corrupt' humour which could
distemper the noble substance of the body, although of course it
is not likely that Shakespeare had only so precise and limited a
meaning in his mind. Nevertheless, the general drift of the
passage would seem to Lemnius or Bright completely in agreement with his own theories.

By 1600 the physical and mental characteristics of at least three
of the four humours had been fairly definitely settled.[32] Next to
the perfect balance, the most favourable complexion was that in
which blood predominated, because blood possessed the vital
qualities of heat and moisture. 'Sanguine' men were of medium
height and inclined to plumpness. Their skins were soft, warm
and smooth; their hair golden or auburn. Their faces were handsome and cheerful, tending towards ruddiness; their eyes blue,
grey or sometimes hazel. Their movements were graceful and
their voices cheerful and melodious. They were healthy, unless
too gross superfluity of blood induced 'lethargy' or apoplexy; if
blood became adust it might result in dangerous fever. In character sanguines were merry, gentle, generous, quick-witted,
brave, amorous and fond of food and drink. Palamon's friend
in *The Two Noble Kinsmen* seems to be of this type:

His complexion
Is (as ripe grape) ruddy: he has felt,
Without doubt, what he fights for, and so apter
To make this cause his owne: In's face appeares
All the fair hopes of what he undertakes,
And when he's angry, then a setled valour
(Not tainted with extreames) runs through his body,
And guides his arme to brave things: Feare he cannot,
He shewes no such soft temper; his head's yellow,
Hard hayr'd, and curl'd, thicke twind like Ivy tods,
Not to undoe with thunder; In his face
The liverie of the warlike Maide appeares,
Pure red, and white, for yet no beard has blest him.
And in his rowling eyes sit victory,

As if she ever ment to court his valour:
His Nose stands high, a Character of honour.
His red lips, after fights, are fit for Ladies.[33]

All Shakespeare's young men might be said in general terms to belong to this complexion, since blood was the humour appropriate to youth. Falstaff has obviously retained into old age the amorousness and gluttony of the sanguine humour, but not its courage and nobility of mind. Prince Henry's description of him as 'that trunk of humours', if it is to be taken as more than a mere item in a catalogue of insults, may refer to the theoretically impossible combination of qualities in his complexion. Sir Toby Belch seems more of a true sanguine; he may come off worse in his encounter with Sebastian, but at least he is not a coward. Anthony is a sanguine of a much higher order; in him the courage, the tendency towards excess and the amorousness of the complexion are raised to heroic pitch. A gross excess of blood led to foolishness and causeless merriment, 'and this', says Bright,

> I take to be the cause of merrie greekes, who seeke rather to discharge themselves of the jocond affection, stirred up by their humour, then require true outward occasion of solace and recreation.[34]

Choleric men were tall, thin and muscular, with much dark hair, usually curled and crisp. They had hawk-noses, brown or yellowish-brown skins and dark, piercing eyes. Their movements were quick and violent, and their voices loud but not sweet. They were particularly subject to fevers, since choler easily became adust through its own heat and turned to morbid melancholy. Their heat made them also much given to lechery. In moderation choler made men bold, valiant, warlike, rash, ambitious and quarrelsome; in gross excess it produced violent, causeless rages, arrogance, envy, jealousy, suspiciousness, discontent, malice and revengefulness. *The Two Noble Kinsmen* again provides us with an idealization of the type:

> He that stands
> In the first place with *Arcite*, by his seeming,
> Should be a stout man, by his face a Prince,
> (His very lookes so say him) his complexion,
> Nearer a browne, than blacke, sterne and yet noble,
> Which shewes him hardy, feareless, proud of dangers:
> The circles of his eyes show fire within him,

And as a heated Lyon, so he lookes;
His haire hangs long behind him, blacke and shining
Like Ravens wings: his shoulders broad and strong,
Armd long and round, and on his Thigh a sword
Hung by a curious Bauldricke, when he frownes
To seal his will with: better, o'my conscience
Was never Souldiers friend.[35]

Marlowe, in Tamburlaine, and Chapman, in Bussy D'Ambois, present two full portraits of the choleric man; Shakespeare's most detailed study is Coriolanus. Katherine the Shrew is obviously of a choleric temperament, and so too is Petruchio, although he exaggerates his choler in order to bring his wife to an amenable state. We may also reasonably attribute this complexion to the quarrelsome soldiers Hotspur, Faulconbridge and Fluellen, to the volatile Mercutio and to the malcontent Cassius. Hotspur is the most interesting of these, for besides the valour, rashness and arrogance of the hot temperature, he shows signs also of vivid imagination. Cassio has a tendency towards choler which shows itself when his brain becomes overheated with wine and the control of his reason is relaxed. Othello and Leontes are both cholerics, but it seems likely that Othello is readily made jealous because of a natural choler indigenous to his race, whereas Leontes is first made jealous and so becomes choleric. This distinction may seem too fine, but it receives some colour from the fact that Leontes never loses command of his reason, while Othello, whose stubborn fiery nature has hitherto found a safe outlet in hardship and battle, is quite consumed with rage when Iago presents him with a cause more intimately related to his own person. Iago's malice (and that of his shadow, Iachimo) may spring from the choler prevalent in their nation, but it might also be regarded by the Elizabethans as a form of melancholy. Lear is obviously of a choleric nature, but here the effect of age has been to render him incapable of satisfying his rage in action, and his mind, unable to find relief for its passions, gives way under the strain.

The phlegmatic was a poor complexion. It made men short, stout, and pursy, with soft, white, hairless, unhealthy skins. Phlegmatics had long, lank hair, sometimes white or straw-coloured, sometimes dead black. Their eyes were protuberant, dull, and watery, and they had poor sight. In movement they

were slow, weak, and ungraceful, and they had weak and tune-
less voices. They were subject to coughs, colds and rheumatic
diseases. In character they were slow, 'lumpish', lazy, dull-
witted, of weak memory, effeminate and cowardly. In their
favour it may be said that they were amiable and sweet-tempered,
but this was only because they lacked the stimulus to become
anything more definite. All women can be assumed to be of
this temperament, unless like Katherine, Beatrice or Cleopatra
they give evidence to the contrary. Cleopatra, who is obviously
of an unusually fiery nature, is delighted to hear that Octavia
cannot rival her in this:

> *Cleo.* Is she tall as me?
> *Mes.* She is not Madam.
> *Cleo.* Didst hear her speake?
> Is she shrill tongu'd or low?
> *Mes.* Madam, I heard her speake, she is low voic'd.
> *Cleo.* That's not so good: he cannot like her long.
> *Char.* Like her? Oh *Isis*: 'tis impossible.
> *Cleo.* I thinke so *Charmian*: dull of tongue and dwarfish.
> What Majestie is in her gate, remember
> If ere thou look'st on Majestie.
> *Mes.* She creepes: her motion, & her station are as one:
> She shewes a body, rather then a life,
> A statue, then a Breather. . . .
> *Cleo.* Bear'st thou her face in mind? is't long or round?
> *Mes.* Round, even to faultinesse.
> *Cleo.* For the most part too, they are foolish that are so. Her haire
> what colour?
> *Mes.* Browne Madam: and her forehead
> As low as she would wish it.[36]

All the qualities which the Messenger enumerates—the low
stature, feeble voice, low forehead and sluggish movements—
are typical of the phlegmatic; Octavia is obviously no match for
the sanguine Anthony. Aguecheek's long, flaxen hair, cowardice
and stupidity suggest a phlegmatic complexion, and so do
Master Slender's yellow beard and general dimness of wit. Cordelia's inability to emulate the ready rhetoric of her sisters might
also be attributed to this cause.

The melancholic was the most complicated of all the complexions. Bright says:

Of all the other humours melancholie is fullest of varietie of passion, both according to the diversitie of place where it setleth . . . as also through the diverse kindes.[37]

An excess of 'natural' melancholy was very unfavourable to health, since its cold and dry nature was directly opposed to the vital qualities of heat and moisture. Melancholiacs suffered a variety of diseases and were always ailing. One of the functions of melancholy was to thicken and cool the blood, which would otherwise become too hot and volatile under the influence of choler. In excess melancholy would, as King John says, 'bake' the blood and make it 'heavy-thick', and all the vital processes would be hindered.[38] An excess of melancholy also disordered the digestion, and in consequence the spirits concocted were foul and dull. Melancholiacs were slow and heavy in movement and gesture; in character, they were surly, taciturn, bad-mannered, unsociable, envious, suspicious, jealous and covetous. They were slow to wrath, but if aroused stubborn and cruel in pursuit of their revenge; amorous, but bashful, timid, and uncouth. Lemnius gives this description of them:

> As touching the notes and markes of their minds, they are churlish, whyning, wayward and ill to please, stubborne, intractable, obstinate, greedy of worldly goods, and covetous of money, pinching and sparing, when they have got it, and not daringe to spend or bestow upon themselves such things, as the necessity of mans life for use requyreth. A man may also know them by their kind of gate: for they use a certain slow pace and soft nyce gate, holding down their heads, with countenaunce and loke so grim / and frowninge, as thoughe they were lately come out of Trophonius denne, or oute of some Cave under the ground (such as the fabulous yawning of the earth in Ireland, commonly tearmed S. Patrickes denne or Purgatorye) is. To conclude, the grimme and surly Planet of Saturne, together wyth Melancholie so disposeth them that (as though they were bound by vow to sylence and taciturnity) a man shall scantly get a word out of their mouthes.[39]

The most pronounced characteristic of melancholiacs, however, was a tendency to causeless fear and sorrow. Burton, following Du Laurens and others, defines Melancholy as:

> a kind of dotage without a fever, having for his ordinary companions fear and sadness, without any apparent occasion.[40]

A 'dotage' was properly speaking a disorder of one or more mental faculties not accompanied by frenzy—that is, a calm madness; 'without a fever' was added to distinguish it from delirium, for which the cold and dry nature of the melancholy humour was unsuited. Melancholy was not always sad, as Bright notices:

> The perturbations of melancholie are for the most part, sadde and fearefull, and such as rise of them: as distrust, doubt, diffidence or dispaire, sometimes furious, and sometimes merry in apparaunce, through a kind of Sardonian, and false laughter, as the humour is disposed that procureth these diversities;[41]

but this was by reason of the effects of some kinds of unnatural melancholy. At the beginning of *The Merchant of Venice*, Antonio is suffering from an apparently causeless sadness:

> In sooth I know not why I am so sad,
> It wearies me: you say it wearies you;
> But how I caught it, found it, or came by it,
> What stuffe 'tis made of, whereof it is borne,
> I am to learne: and such aWant-wit sadnesse makes of mee
> That I have much ado to know myself.[42]

Antonio may be grieving, without admitting it, over the coming departure of Bassanio, or it may be that his prophetic soul is warning him of disasters to come, but we may be sure that if he had taken his trouble to an Elizabethan doctor, the diagnosis would have been a melancholic distemper of the blood, and treatment prescribed accordingly. No doubt he would have been purged, put on a 'light diet' as we should say, and encouraged, like Christopher Sly, to pursue his favourite sports, to hear pleasant music and witness merry plays. A temporary fit of melancholy of this nature was not dangerous, provided it was taken in hand, and indeed it was possible to be constitutionally melancholy without danger:

> All such as we call melancholike men, are not infected with this miserable passion which wee call melancholie; there are melancholike constitutions, which keep without the bounds and limits of health, which if we credit ancient writers, are very large and wide.[43]

As with all the humours, the danger lay in a too violent reaction to a natural stimulus.

It was the causeless fear and sorrow of melancholiacs that

G

caused them to be solitaries, 'wanderers from the herd', like
their prototype Timon. These 'perturbations' were intensified
by the other marked characteristic of melancholiacs, a disturbed
imagination. In *The Method of Physicke*, Barrough defines Melancholy as:

> an alienation of the mind troubling reason, & waxing foolish, so that
> one is almost beside himself. . . . The most common synes be fearful-
> ness, sadnes, hatred, and also they that be melancholious, have
> strange imaginations, for some thinke them selves brute beasts, and
> do counterfait their voice and noise, some thinke themselves / vessels
> of earth, or earthen pots, and therefore they withdraw them selves
> from them that they meete, least they should knock together.[44]

Most writers on Melancholy give lists of melancholic imaginings
of the same kind as those which Barrough mentions; it was
partly because all kinds of hallucination could be included under
it that the term 'melancholy' became so various in meaning.[45]
Religious mania fell in under this head. Boorde, defining 'A
certaine kynd of madnes named Melancholia', says:

> This sicknes is named the melancholy madnesse which is a sickenes
> full of fantasies thynkynge to here or to se that thynge that is not
> harde nor sene, and a man havyng this madnes, shall thynke in hym
> selfe that thynge that can never be, for some be so fantastycall that
> they wyl thynke them selfe God or as goode, or such thynges per-
> teyning to presumption or to desperaccioun to be dampned.[46]

Burton, of course, devotes an entire section of the *Anatomy* to
'religious Melancholy'. One difficulty was to distinguish melancholy from true religious gravity on the one hand, and from the
deadly sin of Accidia or Despair on the other. Timothy Bright,
according to his own account, wrote his *Treatise* in an attempt
to distinguish for the benefit of a friend, between natural melancholy and the 'heavie hand of God upon the afflicted conscience'.[47]

Melancholiacs tended to suffer from insomnia, and if they slept
they experienced horrible dreams. Paré says of them that:

> they are observed to see in the night Devils, Serpents, darke dens and
> caves, sepulchers, dead corpses, and many other such things full of
> horror, by reason of a blacke vapour, diversely moving and disturb-
> ing the Braine.[48]

The visionary faculty was strongly developed in melancholiacs, by reason of their disordered imagination:

> And even as slime and durt in a standing puddle, engender toads and frogs and many other unsightly creatures, so this slimie melancholy humor still thickening as it stands still, engendreth many mishapen objects in our imaginations. . . . Our reason even like drunken fumes it displaceth and intoxicates, & yeelds up our intellective apprehension to be mocked and trodden under foote by everie false object or counterfet noyse that comes neere it.[49]

This was particularly relevant to the question of ghosts and apparitions. Here there was again the familiar division of opinions. Some believed that all such phenomena were genuine supernatural manifestations: others that they were the result of simple failures of the senses, or even of trickery by priests who imposed on the credulity of the vulgar. The middle position was that while some visions were genuine and others fraudulent, still others might be the work of the devil or his minions, taking advantage of a disordered mind.[50] Hamlet is afraid that the Devil may have stimulated his imagination, which is already disturbed by melancholy resulting from grief, to 'project' a false spectre of his dead father. Other apparitions might be the pure product of minds overcome by melancholy. In *The White Devil* there is a striking scene where Duke Francisco, in order to strengthen his desire for revenge, actually calls on his melancholic imagination to summon up a vision of his murdered sister:

> To fashion my revenge more seriously,
> Let me remember my dead sisters face:
> Call for her picture? no; I'le close mine eyes,
> And in a melancholicke thought I'le frame
>
> *Enter Isabella's ghost.*
>
> Her figure 'fore me. Now I ha't—how strong
> Imagination workes! how she can frame
> Things which are not! me / thinks she stands afore me;
> And by the quicke Idea of my minde,
> Were my skill pregnant, I could draw her picture.
> Thought, as a subtile juggler, makes us deeme
> Things, supernatural, which have cause
> Common as sickenes. 'Tis my melancholy—
> How cam'st thou by thy death?—How idle am I

To question mine owne idlenesse! Did ever
Man dream awake till now?—Remove this object;
Out of my brain with't: what have I to do
With tombes, or death-beds, funerals or teares,
That have to meditate upon Revenge?

Exit ghost.

So, now 'tis ended, like an old wives story:
Statesmen think often they see stranger sights
Than madmen.[51]

Later in the play, however, Brachiano's ghost makes a 'genuine'
appearance to Flamineo, who says: 'This is beyond melancholy.'
Shakespeare does not trouble to make it clear whether his ghosts
are 'real' or illusory. The ghost of Hamlet's father is apparently
'genuine', but the ghost of Banquo may only exist in Macbeth's
imagination, as does the visionary dagger. The ghosts that appear
to Richard III before Bosworth appear to be the products of his
guilty conscience, although they speak to Richmond. Richmond, however, is unaware of their presence, and it may be only
in Richard's imagination that they call down blessings on his
rival, and indeed the whole 'show' may be only a dream.
Caesar's ghost calls itself Brutus' 'evil spirit', which may mean
that it is a real ghost come to work evil to Brutus or to warn
him of impending evil, or that it is his evil genius assuming the
shape of Caesar, or that it is a product of his guilty conscience.
Whatever it is, Brutus, like a true Stoic, refuses to be impressed
by it, and treats it in a very cavalier fashion. In this, as in all con-
troversial matters, it was Shakespeare's habit to avoid committing
himself.

Du Laurens gives a moving picture of the woeful state of the
natural melancholiac:

The melancholike man properly so called . . . is ordinarilie out of
heart, alwaies fearfull and trembling, in such sort as that he is afraid
of everything, yea, and maketh himself a terror unto himself, as the
beast which looketh himselfe in a glasse; he would runne away and
cannot goe, he goeth alwaies sighing, troubled with the hicket, and
with an unseparable sadnes, which oftentimes turneth into dispayre:
he is alwaies disquieted both in bodie and spirit, he is subject to
watchfulnesse, which doth consume him on the one side, and unto
sleep, which tormenteth him on the other side; for if he think to

make truce with his passions by taking some rest, behold so soone as hee would shut his eyelids, hee is assayled with a thousand vaine visions, and hideous buggards, with fantastical inventions, and dreadful dreams; if he would call any to helpe him, his speech is cut off before it be half ended, and what he speaketh commeth out in fasting and stammering sort, he can not live with companie. To conclude, hee is become a savadge creature, haunting the shadowed places, suspicious, solitarie, and enemie to the Sunne, and in whom nothing can please, but only discontentment, which forgeth unto itself a thousand false and vaine imaginations.[52]

It is not easy to say whether it was the development of medical theory that led psychologists to distinguish so many kinds of melancholic affliction, or whether it was the use of 'melancholy' to cover all kinds of mental disorder which induced complications in medical theory. Probably the influence was mutual. At all events, by the time that Burton was writing and for some time before (for Burton was a late and derivative student of his subject) the matter had become so involved that one has profound sympathy with his complaint:

> in such obscurity, therefore, variety and confused mixture of symptoms, causes, how difficult a thing it is to treat of several kinds apart; to make any certainty or distinction among so many casualties, distractions, when seldom two men shall be like affected *per omnia*![53]

The first confusion in point of time was between Melancholy and Choler—a confusion which has its source in the original Hippocratic conception of 'black' and 'yellow' bile. The earliest uses of 'melancholy' in English are in the sense of 'wrathful' or 'violent'. Thus Gower notes that of the servants of Wrath, the first

> Malencolie
> Is cleped, which in compaignie
> An hundred times in an houre
> Wol as an angri beste loure
> And noman wot the cause why.[54]

Traces of this association remained with 'melancholy' to the end; they were easily called into play by the association of melancholy with discontent, envy and jealousy.

The corruption or 'adustion' of the different humours pro-

duced different species of melancholy. Thus according to Bright,
putrefaction of the melancholy humour itself caused 'monstrous
terrors and fears and heaviness without cause'.[55] Paré says that
'when Melancholy hath exceeded natures and its owne bounds,

> then by reason of putrefaction and inflammation all things appear
> full of extreme furie and madnesse, so that they often cast themselves
> headlong down from some high place, or are otherwise guilty of
> their own death, with fear of which notwithstanding they are
> terrified.[56]

Corruption of blood produced unnatural levity and carelessness;
corruption of phlegm outrageous storms of weeping, and fascination with the sight of water.[57] Choler, which by reason of its hot,
dry nature was particularly liable to become adust, 'bringeth the
minde into furious fitts, phreneticke rages and brainsicke madness' if it became too much 'enflamed'.[58] That this state could be
called 'melancholy', although by strict definition melancholy
was distinguished from frenzy, is an indication of the confusion
to which a liberal use of the term had given rise. Corruption of
the humours when mixed had still more various results. Corruption of melancholy when mixed with blood made a man (according to Langton) 'merry madde'; if it became adust when mixed
with a little phlegm it made him 'slothfull without all meane or
measure'.[59] Corruption of melancholy mixed with choler produced the worst results:

> and if the cholerike and melancholike humours be corrupte and
> mingled together, their natures become monstrous, proud, full of
> envy, fraud subtilities, venemous and hatefull, poisonful and dia-
> bolical,

says Primaudaye;[60] we may compare Monsieur's characterization of Bussy D'Ambois:

> > thy gall
> Turns all thy blood to poison, which is cause
> Of that toad-pool that stands in thy complexion,
> And makes thee (with a cold and earthy moisture,
> Which is the dam of putrefaction,
> As plague to thy damn'd pride) rot as thou liv'st,
> To study calumnies and treacheries,
> To thy friends' slaughters like a screech-owl sing,
> And do all mischiefs, but to kill the King.[61]

This was the humour most appropriate to envious, villainous malcontents.

The effects of melancholy could also be diverse according to the part of the body in which the humour had 'settled' or had infected. It was customary to distinguish between melancholy of the whole body, melancholy in the head alone, and melancholy in the 'hypochondries' or bowels.[62] Melancholy dispersed through the body at large produced any of the symptoms already described according to the kind and amount of the humour which caused the distemperature. Head melancholy was characterized specifically by the mental symptoms; the sufferer was 'the melancholy man properly so-called' whom Du Laurens describes.[63] Du Laurens adds that if melancholy settling in the head caused the sufferer to avoid society and live savagely like a beast it was called 'wolve's melancholy'. Lycanthropy, from which Duke Ferdinand suffers in *The Duchess of Malfy* was sometimes included under this head.[64] To head melancholy Du Laurens also ascribes 'knight's melancholy', that is, the passion of Love, or Erotomania, sometimes also called 'heroic melancholy'.[65] Hypochondriacal or 'windy' melancholy produced, besides the ever-present causeless fear and sorrow, a sensation of burning in the midriff, flatulence, swelling of the stomach, 'crudities' and 'oppilations' or stoppages—in fact a variety of symptoms answering to disorders ranging from acidity of the stomach to gastric ulcer and cancer.

All in all there was no doubt that the melancholic complexion was a dangerous condition which only too easily assumed the nature of a very serious illness. It is therefore surprising to find that it was regarded as in some ways a desirable state, which certain men would take some pains to simulate. Of course, the affectation of a 'humour' became smart round about the turn of the century. 'Humour' early acquired the sense of 'oddity of character', 'idiosyncrasy' (hence the term 'a humorous part', played by what we should call 'a character actor') and also the sense of 'whim' or 'caprice',[66] and it is in the last sense that it seems chiefly to have become a catchword with the gallants:

> Ask *Humours* why a Feather he doth weare?
> It is his humour, (by the Lord,) heele swear![67]

Jonson made an effort, in the Introduction to *Every Man out of*

his Humour, to stop the degeneration of the term, and to wrest it
to his own meaning:

<blockquote>
So in every Humane body
The choller, melancholy, flegme and bloud
By reason that they flow continually
In some one part, and are not continent,
Receive the name of Humours. Now thus farre
It may, by *Metaphore*, apply it selfe
Unto the general disposition:
As when some one peculiar quality
Doth so possesse a man, that it doth drawe
All his affects, his spirits and his powers,
In their confluctions, all to runne one way.
This may be truly said to be a Humour . . .
</blockquote>

Jonson, in fact, wished to extend the original medical significance of the term and to transform it, in accordance with the
theory of Decorum, into something more like 'master passion'.
This was perhaps a legitimate extension of meaning, and there
is no doubt that Jonson further popularized the term; but he did
not succeed in confining it to his own sense. By the time of *The
Alchemist* (acted 1610), he had apparently given up the struggle
and accepted the looser usage:

<blockquote>
Our *Scene* is *London*, 'cause we would make known,
No country's mirth is better than our owne.
No clime breeds better matter for your whore,
Bawd, squire, imposter, many persons more,
Whose manners, now call'd humors, feed the stage . . .[69]
</blockquote>

In the meantime the fashionable use of the term, with which
we may perhaps compare the modern cant use of 'complex',
continued unabated. Samuel Rowlands, writing at the height of
the craze in 1600, sums it up neatly:

<blockquote>
Humours is late crown'd King of Caueeleres,
Fantastique-follies, grac'd with common favour. . . .
Fashions is still consort with new fond shapes,
And feedeth dayly upon Strange disguise . . .
Thus *Vertu's* hid, with *Follies* juggling mist,
And he's no man, that is no Humourist.[70]
</blockquote>

Melancholy, however, was affected as a humour properly so-
called, and this was not the case with any other humour. The

explanation is to be found in the last of the major problems connected with this complexion, and is in itself a good illustration of the difficulties of the eclectic approach to the authorities. The cold and dry melancholy was directly opposed to the vital qualities, and melancholiacs should therefore be weak, dull and feeble in intellect as well as sickly in body. But Aristotle had said otherwise. In his *Problems* he had raised the question:

> Why is it that all men who are outstanding in Philosophy, Poetry and the Arts are melancholic, and some to such an extent that they are infected by the diseases of the black bile . . .?[71]

If 'The Philosopher' said this it must be true, however hard it was to reconcile it with the other facts; only a very bold man would attempt to deny it. There were various ways of resolving the difficulty. It could be said, for example, that Aristotle was speaking comparatively, and meant only that a certain degree of coldness was necessary to temper the otherwise excessive heat of the Imagination.[72] Weight could be laid on the dryness of Melancholy, which was beneficial to the Understanding; it was customary in this argument to adduce the famous dictum of Heraclitus: 'A dry soul is the wisest and best.'[73] There was some ground for saying that melancholiacs made good scholars, because although their coldness and dryness made them slow to learn, their memory was very retentive.[74] Another way of circumventing the apparent paradox was to say that Aristotle was referring not to natural melancholy, but to melancholy mixed with some other humour, probably blood.[75] Or it might be emphasized that Aristotle was referring specifically to the 'atrabilious' temperament, that is the complexion rising from melancholy of 'choler adust', which was of a hotter and more rarefied nature than natural melancholy. Thus Lemnius first says that an excessive adustion of this humour is dangerous, but adds:

> contrarywyse, when all things consiste within mediocritye, it causeth and bringeth forth sharpnesse of witte, excellency of learning, subtility of invention, eloquence of tongue and right skilful utteraunce, with knowledge howe to speake.[76]

It was also possible to follow Aristotle in noticing that the coldness of melancholy made it hard to ignite, but that if it became warmed, through, perhaps, admixture of adust choler, it quickly became excessively hot. In this way were produced violent transitions from depression to exaltation, which we might recognize as the symptoms of manic depression. Thus Walkington says:

> the melancholike man is said of the wise to be *aut Deus aut Daemon*, either angel of heaven or a fiend of hell, for in whomsoever this humour hath dominion, the soule is either wrapt up into an *Elysium* and paradise of blisse by a heavenly contemplation, or into a direfull hellish purgatory by a cynicall meditation . . .[77]

The last method of resolving the problem was to single out for notice the over-active imagination of melancholiacs, and link with it the Platonic concept of the 'divine enthusiasm' of poets. Aristotle had again pointed the way here, noting of 'black bile' that if it is overheated,

> it produces cheerfulness with song and madness . . . many, because this heat is near to the seat of the mind, are affected by the diseases of madness or frenzy, which accounts for Sibyls, Bacis and all inspired persons.[78]

Du Laurens virtually combines every argument. He begins by rejecting natural melancholy, which, he says, makes men

> fearefull, sluggish and without understanding: it is commonly called Asse-like Melancholie.

He also rejects melancholy adust, which

> doth cause men to be outragious and unfit to be employed in any charge.

The desirable form of melancholy is

> that which is mixed with a certaine quantitie of blood, that maketh men wittie, and causeth them to exceed others. The reasons hereof are very plaine. The braine of such melancholike persons is neither too soft nor too hard, and yet it is true, that dryness doth beare the sway therein. But *Heraclitus* oftentimes said, that a drie light did make the wisest mind: there are but small store of excrements in their braine, their spirits are most pure, and are not easilie wasted, they are hardly drawne from their purpose and meaning; their conceit is very deepe, their memorie very fast, their body strong to endure labour, and when this humour groweth hot, by the vapours of blood, it causeth as it were, a kind of divine ravishment, called

Enthousiasma, which sitrreth men up to plaie the Philosophers, Poets, and also to prophesie: in such maner as that it may seeme to containe in it some divine parts.[79]

Whatever physiological explanation was to be offered for Aristotle's paradox, there were apparently many towards the end of the sixteenth century who were prepared to echo Marston's invocation in the Proemium to *The Scourge of Villainy* (1598):

> Thou nursing mother of fair Wisdom's lore,
> Ingenuous Melancholy, I implore
> Thy grave assistance: take thy gloomy seat,
> Enthrone thee in my blood; let me entreat,
> Stay his quick jocund skips, and force him run
> A sad-paced course . . .[80]

'Melancholicke' became a word of power; it appears in the title of books—for example, Robert Tofte's *The Month's minde of a Melancholicke Lover* (1598), or Nicholas Breton's *Melancholicke Humours in verse of divers natures* (1600). In the association of Melancholy with writing, and particularly with poetry, we may perhaps see a parallel with the present-day conception of the 'neurotic' writer. All creative work, we are told by some, is the product of a neurosis; it is an easy if fallacious step to assume that to be neurotic is to be a writer. There were other reasons why young men anxious to impress should affect melancholy. The melancholiac was not as other men. His gravity and seriousness (only too easily confused with wisdom) marked him off from his light-minded and frivolous contemporaries. He could be assumed to entertain a secret sorrow, most probably, of course, a disappointment in love. Or it might be that his nobler mind was sickened by the deception and frivolity of the world. Marston, acting on a hint from Persius, had identified Melancholy with the noble scorn of satire, and this lead was not overlooked.[81] The melancholiac was thus fitted to occupy two stock positions of the writer in the 1590's: on the one hand, the wounded and reproachful lover of the sonnet sequences, and on the other the jeering intellectual of the satires and epigrams. Again, melancholy was an 'occupational disease', as we should say, among

those that be Magistrates and Officers in the Commonwealth, or Studentes which at unseasonable times sit at their Bookes and Studies. For through overmuch agitation of the mynde, natural heat is ex-

tinguished, and the Spyrits as well Animall as Vitall, attenuated and
vanish away; whereby it commeth to passe, that often their vitall
juyce is exhausted, and they fall into a Colde and Drye constitution.[82]

It was easy to overlook the fact that not all melancholy, even
supposing it was real, came necessarily from so worthy and
dignified a source.

The melancholiac was, in fact, to use words formerly much
loved of lady novelists, 'distinguished' and 'interesting'. Melancholy was also a disease of the gentleman. This was physiologically correct, for this humour was bred by idleness, the badge of
nobility, and had no place in the arduous and healthy life of the
labourer. This point is made as early as Lyly's *Midas* (1589–90).
The pages Petulus and Licio are talking to Motto, the barber:

> *Petulus.* How now, *Motto*, what all a mort?
> *Motto.*   I am as melancholy as a cat.
> *Licio.*   Melancholy? marie gup, is melancholy a word for a barbar's
>   mouth? thou shouldst say, heavie, dull and doltish: melan-
>   choly is the creast of Courtiers armes, and now everie base
>   companion, beeing in his muble fubles, sayes he is melan-
>   choly.[83]

The fantastic Don Armado complains of being 'besieged with
the sable-coloured melancholy' even before he suffers the pangs
of love for Jaquenetta.[84] The most famous examples are the gulls
in *Every Man in his Humour*: Stephen harps on his melancholy to
emphasize his gentility, and Matthew connects it with his
prowess as a poet.[85]

The satirists and epigrammatists of the end of Elizabeth's
reign, and a little later the character writers, were quick to hold
the affectation up to ridicule,[86] and they and the dramatists
provide us with a clear picture of the appearance of the type.
From them we learn of the characteristic suit of black,[87] the
slovenliness,[88] and the large hat pulled well down over the eyes.[89]
We learn also of the pose with the arms folded—a conventional
symbol of grief—and the head sunk down on the breast.[90] The
melancholiac had also his peculiar slow, solemn walk, with
downcast eyes—'carrying his head as if he look'd for pins in the
street'.[91]

The satirists, naturally, present the melancholiacs in no favourable light. The best they can say of them is that they are fishing

> with this melancholly baite
> For this foole Gudgin, this opinion.

—the affectation against which Gratiano counsels Antonio.[92] Nashe hits them off in *Pierce Pennilesse* (1592) with his usual vigour:

> Some think to be counted rare Politicians and Statesmen, by being solitary: as who would say, I am a wise man, a brave man, *Secreta mea mihi: Frustra sapit, qui sibi non sapit;* and there is no man worthy of my companie or friendship: when, although he goes ungartred like a malecontent Cutpursse, & weares his hat over his eies like one of the cursed crue, yet cannot his stabbing dagger, or his nittie love-lock, keep him out of the legend of fantasticall cockscombs. . . . Is it not a pitiful thing that a fellow that eates not a good meales meate in a weeke, but beggereth his belly quite and cleane to make his backe a certaine kinde of brokerly Gentleman . . . should take uppe a scornfull melancholy in his gate and countenance, and talke as though our common welth were but a mockery of government, and our Majestrates fooles, who wronged him in not looking into his deserts, not imploying him in State matters, and that, if more regard were not had of him very shortly, the whole Realme should have misse of him, & he would go (I mary would he) where he should be more accounted of?[93]

This passage brings out the inevitable connection between melancholy and malcontentism. Nashe's subject is merely a poor and stupid pretender to wisdom and dignity, but Nashe indicates that he may be mistaken for a much more sinister figure. There was a link here between the melancholy man and the malcontent traveller, who, as Greene said of himself, returned from the Continent dissatisfied with the state of England and with his own position.[94] There is some evidence to suggest that some acquired the affectation of melancholy abroad, along with other attributes of pseudo-gentility. Certainly some of the dislike of the Frenchified—and still more of the Italianate—Englishmen accreted to the melancholiac. Marston (characteristically) credits the melancholy returned traveller with having brought back little but disease and a taste for un-English vice.[95] More sinister still was the suggestion that the garb of the melancholiac might cover a really dangerous malcontent either in politics or religion—very often, indeed, the same in the

Elizabethan and Jacobean periods. Guilpin suggests this, while denying that his subject is anything more than an unemployed informer:

> But see yonder
> One like the unfrequented Theater
> Walks in darke silence a vast solitude,
> Suited to those blake fancies which intrude,
> Upon possession of his troubled breast:
> But for black's sake he would look like a jeast
> For he's cleane out of fashion: whaťs he? . . .
> Would you needs know? He is a malcontent:
> A papist? No, nor yet a Protestant,
> But a discarded Intelligencer . . .[96]

Writing later, Robert Anthony suggests that the melancholy student, disappointed of preferment here, may attempt to subvert the state from overseas:

> And yet *Philosophers* affirmed thus,
> That *Saturnists* were most ingenious;
> Who long retaine their great *Italian-hate*,
> Wittie in nothing, but things desperate;
> To glut revenge, with studious memorie
> Of shallow *wrongs*, or some slight *injurie* /
> Which if this be his wit to study *ill*,
> Take my *wits* mad-man, leave me *simple still*:
> Under this *dogged Starre*, th'infected moode
> Of discontented *Graduates*, hatch thir *broode*,
> Flying like *swallowes* from the *winters* frost
> To warme *preferment*, in a forren *coast*;
> And there vent all their long-digested *hate*,
> In *scandalous volumes* 'gainst the *King* and *State*.[97]

Masters Stephen and Matthew, and all who copied their attempts to simulate dignified, sober and intellectual melancholy, were laying themselves open to grave misinterpretation.

Besides being the first to make a definite link between the melancholy man and the satirist, Marston appears to be the first to have put a character on the stage who embodies the combination. Feliche, although he has no integral part in the action of *Antonio and Mellida* (acted 1599) is a fairly well-defined portrait of a sober-minded contemner of Court luxury, vice and flattery.

His nature mingles elements of the melancholiac, the stoic and the cynic. He sums himself up in the line:

I envy none, but hate, or pity all.[98]

With him may be classed Dowseger, the melancholy philosopher of Chapman's *A Humorous Day's Mirth* (also 1599), although this is a rather vague sketch. Macilente is a harder, altogether very Jonsonian version of the type: he is sufficiently characterized before the play opens:

> A man well parted, a sufficient Scholler, and travail'd; who (wanting that place in the worlds account, which he thinks his merit capable of) falls into such an envious apoplexie, with which his judgement is so dazeled, and distasted, that he growes violently impatient of any opposite happinesse in another.[99]

Shakespeare softened the lines of this 'humour', making it both more poetic and more human, in Jaques, with his love of solitude, his lack of inner harmony (his nature is 'compact of jars'), his quick scorn for folly, his bent for satire, his pity and his philosophizing. Jaques is both satirical and satirized; he has a dual value as provoking laughter at others as well as at himself. Like Feliche, he is not essential to the play in which he finds himself, but he may stand as the complete type of the intellectual, poetic melancholiac without any of the sinister overtones which the complexion tended to acquire.[100]

It is uncertain whether Marston also deserves the credit for the further step of identifying the melancholiac and the revenge hero —a step easily made through the element of malcontentism common to both. *The Malcontent* is hardly a revenge play by strict definition, for the revenge which Malevole intends to take on Pietro is psychological, and although deaths are plotted, and some are feigned, no blood is actually shed. Indeed *The Malcontent* might be regarded as a tragicomedy. Malevole, however, is certainly a malcontent, and to that extent at least, a melancholiac. Moreover he deliberately plays the part of the satirical melancholiac, or what he himself calls 'the free-breathed malcontent', and is so taken by the other characters, particularly by the usurper Pietro. He comments on the advantage this disguise gives him in allowing him to speak his mind without arousing suspicion—indeed, so winning a reputation for plain-dealing.[101] In this he has a link with 'honest' Iago.

Since we are uncertain of the dates of composition of both plays, we cannot tell whether the character of Hamlet owes anything to that of Malevole or not.[102] Shakespeare had certainly drawn a rough sketch of the melancholy malcontent in the person of Don John before Marston wrote *The Malcontent*.[103] In any case, Hamlet possesses almost all of the characteristics of the melancholy man as that figure was understood about 1600. His natural 'complexion', if we are to judge from Ophelia's account of him, was either balanced or sanguine—at all events a favourable one. This, we may assume, has been temporarily converted to a melancholic 'distemper' by grief at the death of his father. To this 'adventitious' melancholy may also have contributed discontent at being passed over in the succession, disgust at his mother's second marriage, and possibly something of the scholar's and lover's melancholy. To all this the Elizabethan might reasonably ascribe his philosophizing (and particularly his reflections on death), his world-weariness, his love of solitude, and his quick sarcasm. The announcement of his father's murder lays on him the duty of revenge. It could be argued that this, coming on top of his previous melancholy, further disturbs the balance of his mind, making him, in some degree, mad. It seems, however, more likely that he chooses, like Malevole, to put on an 'antic disposition', and assumes the guise of the satirical melancholiac. It is in this role that he scorns Ophelia, mocks Polonius and Osric, and out-roars Laertes. In these scenes we, with our more delicate susceptibilities, have to remember the Elizabethan dramatic convention that a disguised man *becomes* the character he assumes, and to remember also that Hamlet is engaged in a fight for his life and his honour. Our difficulty, of course, is that we are confronted with a character who to advance his purposes, exaggerates traits already in essence present in his 'true' nature. It is not in consequence easy to say what is 'the real Hamlet' and what not.

There is a further, and still more debatable question—the question of whether, if at all, a melancholic disposition will explain Hamlet's delay in carrying out his revenge. It may, of course, not be necessary to seek an explanation of this in Hamlet's character. The problem can be solved (on one level, at least) by reference to the difficulty (which Laertes' abortive attempt illustrates) of assassinating a powerful and anointed king; to Hamlet's desire to be sure he has just cause, and, once assured, to exact full retribution; to his wish to convince others that his deed of blood was honourable, and not merely motivated by ambition; and finally to his natural desire to escape the retribution which overtakes revengers along with all shedders of blood. Since Coleridge, however, the majority of critics have seen in Hamlet, if not a fatal infirmity of purpose, at least an alternation between violent and unscrupulous activity and morbid reflection. It is indeed possible to justify this interpretation by reference to contemporary accounts of melancholy, but only because the term was so liberally used. Justification could be found for calling almost any unusual mental state 'melancholic'; the proof of that lies in *The Anatomy of Melancholy* itself. For that matter, Aristotle described, in his discussion of the problem already referred to, something approaching the cycle of manic depression which has been seen in Hamlet.[104] On the other hand, most Elizabethan writers would say that a melancholiac by a strict definition was slow to arouse in any cause, but once moved very tenacious in the execution of his purpose, and this would fit Hamlet's actions well enough.[105] To say that Hamlet vacillates in his purpose would suggest to an Elizabethan that he was either a fool or a madman, and a true melancholiac is neither.[106] There is no evidence that melancholiacs were averse to shedding blood; that would be the mark of a phlegmatic coward—for example, Calyphas in the second part of *Tamburlaine*.[107] In any case, Hamlet never says that he has scruples about his revenge, provided that he has just cause. Hamlet is certainly a melancholiac, but it cannot be too much emphasized that his melancholy is Elizabethan and not Romantic; nor is it very profitable to attempt to justify from contemporary psychology whatever critics have inferred about his nature. It seems most likely that when Shakespeare came to re-write the old play of *Hamlet* he found his hero described as 'melancholy', with reference only to his grief at his father's death, and possibly also to his discontent at being supplanted as King by his uncle. Writing about the turn of the century, Shakespeare may well, perhaps not entirely of set purpose, have expanded this hint into a character sketch of the melancholy man as he was popularly understood at that time, without being too

H

careful to ensure that his new intellectual and introspective hero
—at once poetic and philosophical, cynical and idealistic—fitted
exactly into a framework intended for a young and princely
revenger. Subsequent criticism has fastened onto and exploited
the discrepancies thus produced.

Webster repeats the satirical malcontented melancholiac in the
persons of Flamineo in *The White Devil* (? acted 1608–9) and
Bosola in *The Duchess of Malfy* (? acted 1612–3). Flamineo self-
confessedly 'feigns a mad humour' in order to 'keep off questions'.[108] In pursuit of this aim he has a scene with the malcontent Count Lodowick in Webster's best vein of the comic
macabre. He is the best example outside Shakespeare of the
dramatic value of this type of character, who can comment on
the action, poke fun at other characters while himself being
comic, and all the time retain in the audience a sense of his underlying seriousness. Bosola is a slightly different figure. He is ex-
pressly said to be suffering from melancholy. This appears to be
merely malicious envy arising from disappointment, but a hint
is given that it may have arisen from excessive study.[109] He
adopts the pose of the outspoken man—'know you not I am the
blunt soldier?'[110]—apparently, like Hamlet and Iago, partly as a
disguise for his purpose, and partly in order to express his real
thoughts without danger. (Antonio accuses him of maintaining
it in order not to seem 'pufft-up' with his preferment.)[111] This
disguise pays its best dividends in Scene 2 of Act III, where he
defends Antonio against the flatterers who have turned against
him and is rewarded by having the secret of the Duchess'
marriage entrusted to him. Attacks on flattery were part of the
stock-in-trade of the malcontent. Either as part of his pose or as
an expression of his real feelings he attacks the viciousness and
frailty of woman, in the first two scenes of Act III. Such attacks
were again the common property of malcontents—and of course
the verse satirists of the period. Bosola is, however, reluctant to
undertake the work for which he is employed by Ferdinand,
and suffers the stings of conscience, and this makes him in some
ways a more subtle character than Iago. All in all he appears
mainly an Iago-type character with touches of Hamlet in his
composition. Both he and Flamineo dwell much on death, but
this is so common in Webster's characters than one is uncertain
whether it may be taken as another sign of melancholy. The

associations of melancholy gave especial scope to Webster's peculiar ability to combine the poetic, the sardonic and the horrific.

Many other characters in Elizabethan and Jacobean drama are spoken of as 'melancholic'. Most of these are suffering straightforwardly from grief, often as a result of unhappy love. Others are malicious or malcontented, or both, but these are rather on the fringe of the type. Iago, for example, might be regarded by some as melancholic (although he is not actually called so), but if so his melancholy merely takes the form of envy and villainy, concealed behind the pose of the blunt soldier. It is not profitable to pursue the search for melancholiacs too far.[112] In *Timon of Athens* Shakespeare drew a portrait of a melancholiac of a different order—indeed one of the archetypal heroes of melancholy. Timon's earlier foolish generosity and refusal to face facts look like the result of an over-sanguine temperament, which the loss of his fortune and the discovery of the falsity of his friends turns to melancholy. Apemantus makes the point that Timon's melancholy is adventitious:

> This is in thee a Nature but infected,
> A poor unmanly Melancholly sprung
> From change of fortune . . .[113]

(Apemantus, like his colleague Thersites, might himself be regarded as a melancholiac, but the two are probably rather to be thought of as degenerates—outcasts and buffoons with the true dog-like view of life.) Regarded in this light, Timon's story forms a kind of moral interlude, on a theme similar to that of Skelton's *Magnificence*. The moral pointed is the vanity of worldly pleasures and the frailty of human friendships. Timon is never really sane; he goes from wild credulity to complete misanthropy. As Apemantus says of him again, he never attains the golden mean:

> The middle of humanity thou never knewest,
> But the extremitie of both ends.[114]

His instability is contrasted with the constancy of Flavius, the just steward, who, like Horatio, is not a pipe for Fortune's finger to play upon. Timon is essentially the fool of Fortune. In his misanthropy, Timon can see nothing in the world but falseness and bestiality, and wish for nothing but the subversion of all order, civil, moral and natural. Ultimately he may be assumed to have fallen into the deadly sin of Despair. Although the religious aspect of his final state is not developed—it would in any case hardly be appropriate to a classical character—he does in fact commit the final crime of self-murder. Timon is in many ways a truer portrait of the melancholy man as the psychologist (and the theologian) understood him, while Hamlet has more of the popular and literary qualities of the type. Neither, of course, is a melancholiac and nothing more, and neither is a perfect example of the humour. (Neither, for example, has the causeless fears which were supposed to attach to the condition.) Nevertheless, they do embody much of what was understood by 'melancholy', and both portraits—it hardly needs saying—are infinitely superior to anything in the same *genre* produced by any other contemporary writer.

The consideration of the melancholic complexion has led us outside the bounds of psychology narrowly defined. This was unavoidable when a psychological type (or group of types) took such hold on the popular and the literary mind. There remains the question whether there was a vein of genuine melancholy in the life of the period which extends for roughly ten years on either side of the turn of the century. Many writers have maintained that there was, and have attributed it to political causes (particularly to the failure of the Essex rebellion, and to disgust with the character of James I and his court); to religious unrest, counting with that the unsettling effect of the 'new Philosophy', in the various senses in which that rather vague phrase can be interpreted; to discontent among unemployed intellectuals; to the spread of syphilis and even to indigestion and toothache. There is no doubt that there was great interest in the condition both among academic and among popular writers. As far as academic interest—among physicians, psychologists, philosophers and theologians—is concerned, it must be remembered that this is one aspect of a more widespread interest in Man, and that in turn this was part of the more vivid interest which the Renaissance took in all knowledge. Moreover, as has already been pointed out, the term 'melancholy' became used to cover all kinds of mental abnormality and it is unrealistic to quote statements about 'melancholy' as if they all referred to one sharply-defined condition. Many of the symptoms which the Elizabethans associated with the term would seem to us not at

all appropriate. Again, it is a fact that there are more accounts of
mental illness during this period than in the Middle Ages. In the
first place, however, this is true (taking Europe as a whole) from
about 1500 onwards; and in the second, it may argue only more
knowledge, wider diffusion of information, and greater skill in
diagnosis. There are more case-histories of mental illness to be
found in the twentieth century than in the nineteenth, but I imagine we should prefer to attribute this to a similar increase of
psychological knowledge and not to accept the suggestion that
we are more neurotic than our grandparents. The fact that detailed accounts of melancholy are not found in this country until
about 1580 is merely another example of England's backward-
ness in scientific matters as compared with the Continent. (The
genuine student of the subject, of course, would read the Contin-
ental treatises in the original—that is, in Latin.) All the academic
evidence permits us to say is that more interest was taken in
various kinds of mental abnormality in the later Renaissance,
and that this interest was not confined to one country or to a
limited period.

We have also seen a more popular interest in the melancholy
man evinced by the satirist and dramatist. Something must be
allowed here for literary fashion, but there is too great a concord
in the versions of the melancholiac found in satire and on the
stage for him to be dismissed as a purely literary figure. It must
be noticed, however, that the satirists are unanimous in assuming
that the melancholy man was a gull or a rogue who affected his
condition, although this is not true rather later with the character
writers. On the stage the melancholiac appears as a subject for
laughter (even if sympathetic laughter), or with the sinister con-
notations of the malcontent and the revenger. There is little to
suggest that the condition was felt to be inevitable or indeed
particularly appropriate to the time, in the way that young intellectuals to-day seem to consider *angst* as their birth-right. And,
of course, the melancholy man was only one of a number of
stock figures who reappear frequently in satire and satirical
drama; we may feel that he has more significance than the brag-
gart soldier or the lecherous old man, but he is in essence a being
of their order.

We have finally to consider the 'tone' of the writing of the
period, and this is very much a matter of personal feeling. What

may seem to one reader a very profound expression of deep pessimism may seem to another purely conventional or even ironic. There can, however, be no doubt that there is a vein of sadness and seriousness running through Elizabethan lyric poetry from the time of Wyatt and Surrey. From its beginnings, too, the drama evinced a capacity for taking a tragic view of life— although whether this should be termed 'melancholic' might be disputed. From 1593 onwards a very strong note of cynicism, realism and satire makes itself heard, and this was certainly connected by the writers of the time with 'melancholy' in their sense. To go beyond this, and to join together aspects of Shakespeare, Donne, Webster, and perhaps Browne, into a composite picture of 'Jacobean melancholy' seems to me unhistorical. Webster may be in some ways a typical Jacobean; so was Ben Jonson, and no one as far as I am aware has yet called Jonson melancholy. Donne may have been plunged into gloom by the threat of the 'new philosophy', but Bacon, who knew far more about it than Donne, was on the contrary possessed by a great hope for the future of mankind. Sir Thomas Browne was a learned man who was much interested in Death: his contemporary Milton was a still more learned man who in the face of great disaster retained a stubborn faith in Eternal Life. Judicious selection will enable a critic to reconstruct a period almost as he wishes, but the truth is always more complex than such reconstructions suggest.

Ultimately we lack the evidence for a sound conclusion. We have practically nothing of the direct evidence—diaries, letters, autobiographies—with which later ages provide us. There was much in the Elizabethan and Jacobean (as in all) periods which might have made men melancholy; no doubt there were then, as there are now, men whose natural disposition was gloomy. It is safe to say that the interest in the melancholic condition at the end of the sixteenth century led to a fashionable pose of melancholy, assumed perhaps only by a few and for a short time. The fact that it was felt as a pose argues that the mood was not general, and may perhaps even argue that the prevailing mood of the time was cheerful. There would be little point in attempting to achieve distinction by pretending to a condition which was generally shared. At all events, the evidence does not seem to entitle us to believe that the Melancholy man was the symbol of his Age.

Chapter Five

THE SOUL'S EFFECT ON THE BODY

THE consideration of the Soul's effect on the Body reduces itself largely to a consideration of the physical effects of the Passions. It was generally held that the movements of the Rational soul were not accompanied by any bodily change, although they might result in considered action. The Sensitive Soul, however, was more nearly connected with bodily function, and the Passions—the most important aspect of the Sensitive Soul—were by definition both mental and physical phenomena. The Passions were, in fact, the most powerful of the six Non-Natural Things:

> For though we live in a sweet and pure aire, observe a strict diet, use sleepe and exercise according to the rules of Physicke, and keepe fit times and measure in expelling superfluities out of our bodies; yet if we have not quiet, calme and placable mindes, we shall subject our selves to / those diseases that the minde, yeelding to these passions, commonly inflicteth upon the body: these are many in number, grievous to suffer, and dangerous to life.[1]

Violent passion could therefore be spoken of as a disease, without undue straining after metaphor. Thus in *Every Man in his Humour*, Thorello, suspecting his wife of infidelity, tells her (as Othello tells Desdemona) that he is suffering from a pain in the forehead. She says she fears that he is suffering from 'this newe disease', and he answers:

> A new disease? I know not, new or old,
> But it may well be call'd poore mortals Plague;
> For like a pestilence it doth infect
> The houses of the braine: first it begins
> Solely to worke upon the fantasie,
> Filling her seat with such pestiferous aire,
> As soone corrupts the judgement, and from thence,
> Sends like contagion to the memorie,

> Still each of other catching the infection,
> Which as a searching vapour spreads itselfe
> Confusedly through every sensive part,
> Till not a thought or motion in the mind
> Be free from the blacke poison of suspect.[2]

The passions could directly affect the temperature of the body. Anger was regularly defined as 'a boiling of the blood about the heart' and in this passion men did in fact become 'hot-blooded'. Similarly in fear the blood literally 'ran cold'. But the gravest physical effects of the passions were caused by their effect on the heart itself. They caused the heart to expand and contract, sometimes violently, and this together with the consequent movement of the spirits and humours about the body, had severe repercussions on the health. Wright explains that Joy is a healthful passion, because it causes the heart to expand and engender great abundance of 'most purefied spirits',

> which after being dispersed thorow the body, cause a good concoction to be made in all partes, helping them to expel the superfluities; they also cleare the braine, and consequently, the understanding. . . . From good concoction, expulsion of superfluities, and aboundance of spirites, proceedeth a good colour, a clear countenance, and an universall health of the body.[3]

Joy in fact could be regarded as an exercise of the mind with results as beneficial as exercise of the body. Wright goes on, however, to warn the reader that excessive mirth may overheat the blood, and turn to choler. A more serious danger was that sudden and violent joy might cause present death:

> for immoderate and unaccustomed joy, carries so violently the bloud and spirits from the heart, unto the habit of the body, that sodaine and unlookt for death ensues, by a speedy decay of the strength, the lasting fountaine of the vitall humour being exhausted. Which thing principally happens to those who are less heartie, as women and old men.[4]

In *Antonio's Revenge* the death of Andrugino (who has in fact been poisoned) is reported to have come about in this way:

> The vast delights of his large sudden joys
> Open'd his powers so wide, that's native heat
> So prodigally flow'd to th'exterior parts

That th'inner citadell was left unmann'd,
And surpris'd on the sudden by cold death.[5]

In grief the heart contracted and became heavy:

> The cause why sadness doth so moove the forces of the body, I take
> to be, the gathering together of much melancholy blood about the
> heart, which collection extinguishes the good spirits, or at least
> dulleth them; besides, the heart being possessed by such an humour,
> cannot digest as well the blood and spirites, which ought to be dis-
> persed thorow the whole body, but converteth them into melan-
> choly, the which humour being cold and drie, dryeth the whole
> body, and maketh it wither away, for colde extinguisheth heate, and
> drynesse moysture, / which two qualities principally concerne life.[6]

This gathering of melancholy blood about the heart is 'that
perillous stuffe / Which weighs upon the heart' from which
Lady Macbeth's doctor is powerless to free her.[7] Grief made
those whom it afflicted melancholy: they suffered the disorders
of melancholiacs. Thus in Chapman's *Monsieur D'Olive* the Earl
of St. Anne describes his sufferings after the loss of his wife:

> with all which
> I feel in these deep griefs, to which I yield
> (A kind of false, sluggish, and rotting sweeetness
> Mix'd with an humour where all things in life
> Lie drown'd in sour, wretched, and horrid thoughts)
> The way to cowardly desperation opened;
> And whatsoever urgeth souls accurs'd
> To their destruction, and sometimes their plague,
> So violently gripes me, that I lie
> Whole days and nights bound at his tyrranous feet,
> So that my days are not like life or light,
> But bitterest death, and a continual night.[8]

The coldness and dryness of melancholic grief was very dangerous to health; Coeffeteau says that when they come to open those
that have been 'smothered with melancholy',

> instead of a heart, they find nothing but a drie skinne like to leaves
> in Autumn.[9]

A sudden, violent grief would bring about death, for the sudden
rush of blood to the heart 'strangled' it. A death such as that of

the Countess of Gloucester's at the end of Peele's *Edward I* is thus not purely a dramatic convention.[10]

Joy and Grief were from this point of view the two archetypal passions, and all the rest contained some admixture of them. In Fear, as in Grief, the heart contracted, and became weakened. Heat was withdrawn from the rest of the body to comfort the heart, blood and spirits were drawn to it,

> and ther followeth a generall paleness and colde in all the outward parts, and chiefly in the face, with a shivering throughout the whole body . . .[11]

Thus is produced the paleness which so infuriates Macbeth in the messenger who brings news of the advance of the English forces:

> The divell damne thee blacke, thou cream-fac'd Loone:
> Where got'st thou that Goose-looke . . .
> Go pricke thy face, and over-red thy feare
> Thou Lilly-liver'd Boy. What Soldiers, Patch?
> Death of thy Soule, those Linnen cheekes of thine
> Are Counsailers to feare. What Soldiers Whay-face?[12]

The coldness of Fear brings about 'goose-flesh', and the hair stands on end

> because the heate and bloud are returned to the inner parts, and the utmost parts are more cold and drie then stone: by reason whereof the utmost skinne and the pores, in which the rootes of the haires are fastened, are drawne together.[13]

Once again, death might ensue from a violent attack of the passion:

> Yea it commeth to passe sometimes, that present death followeth a great and suddeine feare, because all the bloud retiring to the heart choketh it, and utterly extinguisheth naturall heat and the spirits . . .[14]

Anger was another passion with very powerful effects:

> For first of all when the heart is offended, the bloud boyleth round about it, and the heart is puffed up: whereupon followeth a continuall panting and trembling of the heart and breast.

These 'burning flames and kindled spirits' then ascend to the brain, and distemper that organ also:

from hence cometh change of countenaunce, shaking of the lippes, and of the whole visage, stopping of speech and such other terrible lookes to beholde, more meete for a beaste then for a man.[15]

This passion quickly made itself visible:

a man transported with *Choler* gives great signes of the frenzie that doth afflict him: his eyes full of fire and flame which this *Passion* doth kindle, seeme fiery and sparckling: his face is wonderfully inflamed as by a certaine refluxe of blood, which ascends from the heart: his haire stands upright and staring with horror, his mouth cannot deliver his words: his tongue falters, his feet and hands are in perpetuall motion.[16]

The Elizabethan actor would need considerable skill to satisfy a critical audience in the portrayal of this passion. Primaudaye notices that since Anger is a mixed passion, compounded of grief at a discomfiture and desire or hope for revenge, it can have two effects on the countenance. Some men become pale when they are angry because blood runs to the heart, as it does in grief and sorrow, and such men are the most dangerous. (Richard II goes pale with anger in his interview with the dying John of Gaunt.[17]) Others go red in the face because the blood ascends to the head, and these are not so much to be feared. In any case the heart is not contracted as it is in grief and fear; instead it beats violently and the blood and spirits are dispersed through the body.

Burning of the heart in anger is several times referred to by Shakespeare.[18] We may imagine Richard II and Coriolanus using the same 'action'—tearing the doublet open at the breast— to express the sensation of swelling of the heart which anger also produces:

Swell'st thou prowd heart? Ile give thee scope to beat,
Since Foes have scope to beat both thee and me . . .

Measureless Lyar, thou has made my heart
Too great for what containes it . . .[19]

Titus Andronicus refers to the angry palpitation or 'leaping' of the heart, and so do Lear and Leontes:

Oh how this Mother swels up towards my heart!
Histerica passio, downe thou climbing sorrow,
Thy Elements below . . .

> I have *Tremor Cordis* on me: my heart daunces,
> But not for joy: not joy . . .[20]

These passages seem to refer to the 'mother', of which Jorden says:

> This disease is called by diverse names amongst our Authors. *Passio Hysterica, Suffocatio, Praefocatio,* and *Strangulatus uteri, Caducus matricis,* etc. In English the Mother, or the Suffocation of the Mother, because most commonly it takes them with a choaking in the throat: and it is *an affect of the Mother or wombe* . . .[21]

Hysteria of this kind could be produced by excess passion among other causes, and palpitations of the heart were among its symptoms. It was considered (naturally) most appropriate to women.

Inward heat and swelling of the heart connect Anger with Courage and Pride. Primaudaye says of proud people:

> for holding of the nature of fire, which alwaies ascendeth upward, if they follow their naturall inclination, they will take also of the nature thereof, aspiring continually unto high matters.[22]

This vividly recalls the character of Tamburlaine. Primaudaye also notes that their hot character makes them arrogant, quick and unstable, and Bright shows that they literally suffered from a proud or 'high' stomach:

> their natures for the most parte are troubled with a Cholericke humour, or fretting, like to Choler, about the mouth of the stomach, which is of all the inwarde partes of quickest sense or feeling. This causeth them, especially fasting, before the humour be mitigated, and delayed with nourishment, to be most prone to that angry passion.[23]

Arrogant men also have a 'puffed-up heart', which causes them to boast:

> For pride being nothing els but winde that puffeth up the heart (even as fire causeth water to swel and sent forth great waumes) if the proud man should not find some issue for this winde, he would burst asunder.[24]

Anger was a passion which besides being very powerful to disturb the harmony of the soul, was very dangerous to the health of the body. Paré says that:

> the spirits and humours are so inflamed by it, that it often causes putrid feavers, especially if the body abound with any ill humor.[25]

The King of Soria threatens Tamburlaine with the consequences of his unbridled Pride and Anger:

> May never spirits, vaine or Artier feed
> The cursed substance of that cruel heart,
> But (wanting moisture and remorsefull blood)
> Drie up with anger, and consume with heat;[26]

and Tamburlaine's death does in fact come about in this way, as his physician makes plain:

> Your vaines are full of accidentall heat,
> Whereby the moisture of your blood is dried . . .
> Your Artiers which alongst the vaines convey
> The lively spirits which the heart ingenders
> Are parcht and void of spirit, that the soule
> Wanting those Organnons by which it mooves,
> Can not indure by argument of art.[27]

The heart might literally burst with Anger, as it might with Pride:

> *Choler* doth not only disfigure the body, but many times it ruines it wholly: for some being extraordinarily moved, have broken their veines, and vomited out their soule with the blood.[28]

The desire for Revenge, if it were not satisfied, could have similar results:

> For a man in such a case is not much unlike to a madde dog. For because revenge cannot take that effect which it would have, it vexeth and closeth up as it were the heart, bringing great grief and torment to the whole body, so that a man so affected is as if his heart and body were ready to burst asunder.[29]

The physical effects of Love might be almost as serious:

> by reason of these perturbations of the mind, the bloud becomes adust, earthy, and Melancholy . . . by which meanes diverse have fallen into strange and desperate diseases, growing Melancholy, Foolish, Mad, Cynicall, Wolvish . . .[30]

Love was in fact one of the chief causes of Melancholy: Burton devotes the major part of the Third Partition of the *Anatomy* to it. It could be regarded as a species of melancholy in itself, the so-called 'Heroic melancholy'.[31] It was obvious that unhappy love plunged the sufferer into the depths of violent grief: descriptions of the despised lover are often interchangeable with those of the melancholiac. But even successful lovers were subject to extreme physical stresses. Coeffeteau notes some of the effects on the appearance of the lover:

> for that his soule that loves intirely, is perpetually imployed in the contemplation of the party beloved, and hath no other thoughts but of his merit, the heate, abandoning the parts, and retiring into / the braine leaves the whole body in great distemperature, which corrupting and consuming the whole bloud, makes the face grow pale and wanne, causeth the trembling of the heart, breeds strange convulsions, and retires the spirits in such sort as he seemes rather an image of death, then a living creature.[32]

The lover thus assumed some of the appearance of the sufferer from Grief or Fear. Angelo thus describes his condition while he is awaiting the arrival of Isabella:

> oh heavens
> Why doe's my bloud thus muster to my heart,
> Making it both unable for it selfe,
> And dispossessing all my other parts
> Of necessary fitness?
> So play the foolish throngs with one that swounds,
> Come all to help him, and so stop the ayre
> By which he should revive: and even so
> The generall subject to a wel-wisht King
> Quit their owne part, and in obsequious fondnesse
> Crowd to his presence, where their un-taught love
> Must needs appear offence . . .[33]

An even more extreme state into which the lover was prone to fall was that of ecstasy, which Coeffeteau describes as:

> a true alienation of the sences, which ariseth, for that the spirit and the will of him that loveth, being wholly imployed in the contemplation and enjoying of the thing beloved, suffereth himself to be so transported with this content, as the soule remaines as it were quencht and without motion.[34]

This state, which Donne describes in *The Extasie,* is akin to the mood of religious exaltation in which the soul is rapt in the contemplation of the Divine Idea. Troilus seems to fear that he will fall into this condition when he is awaiting Cressida:

> I am giddy; expectation whirles me round,
> Th'imaginary relish is so sweete,
> That it inchants my sence: what will it be
> When that the watry pallats taste indeede
> Loves thrice repured Nectar? Deathe I feare me
> Sounding distruction, or some joy too fine,
> Too subtile, potent, and too sharpe in sweetnesse,
> For the capacitie of my ruder powers . . .[35]

The acute physical effects which the passion was believed to produce make it less remarkable that lovers in medieval and renaissance romance are so apt to swoon. These effects were aggravated by the proneness of Love to give rise to mixed passions, in which the soul suffered a double stress. The most powerful of these mixed passions was Jealousy, which contained a mixture of Love and Hate. Jealousy not only totally disrupted the calm of the mind, but wasted the body and flooded it with choler. The type of the jealous man was Malbecco:

> Ne ever is he wont on ought to feed,
> But toades and frogs, his pasture poysonous,
> Which in his cold complexion do breed
> A filthy bloud, or humour rancorous,
> Matter of doubt and dread suspitious,
> That doth with cureless care consume the hart,
> Corrupts the stomacke with gall vitious,
> Croscuts the liver with internall smart,
> And doth transfixe the soul with deathes eternall dart.[36]

Another mixed passion from which lovers were very apt to suffer was Shame, a mixture of Anger and Fear. If Fear was the stronger, the sufferer turned pale; if Anger,

> the bloud runnes violently to the face, the eyes look red, and sometimes they fome at the mouth.[37]

Shamefastness was a mild version of this, common in girls and young boys, who turned first pale and then blushed when embarrassed. In its most violent form it became what Paré calls an 'agonie', which might bring about death. It was perfectly possible, in fact, to 'die of shame'. It was also possible for the soul to be possessed by two contradictory passions; the lover, for example, might be torn between Hope and Fear. Such a conflict would impose a great strain on the heart, and would quickly

exhaust the spirits. In *King Lear*, Gloucester dies when his heart
is subject to the violently opposed stresses of Joy and Grief:

> But his flaw'd heart
> (Alacke too weake the conflict too support)
> 'Twixt two extremes of passion, joy and greefe,
> Burst smilingly.[38]

The dangers of excessive passion made it essential that the
heart should if possible be relieved. The two most immediate
and natural ways of relief were sighs and tears. The function of
sighs was easily apparent:

> Sighing has no other cause of moving then to coole and refresh the
> heart, with fresh breath, and pure ayre, which is the nourishment and
> foode of the vitall spirites, besides the cooling which the heart it selfe
> receiveth thereby.[39]

In some passions sighing and sobbing was in any case an involun-
tary result of the outrageous beating of the heart. There appears
to be no medical support for Shakespeare's belief, to which he
several times refers, that sighs and tears wasted the blood; this
must be based on some popular tradition.[40] Tears are equally
easily accounted for. According to Bright, they are 'an excre-
mentitious humiditie of the braine' which is normally voided by
the palate and the nose. When, as in Grief and Terror, the blood
and spirits rush to the heart, and the body as it were contracts,
the tears are squeezed out of the brain as water is squeezed from
a sponge. In excessive Grief and Fear, however, the watery
humour of tears is also drawn inwards; the pores are shut, and
the sufferer is beyond crying. Bright also explains how tears are
shed for joy; the general expansion of the spirits which accom-
panies pleasure forces them out of the brain.[41] It is also possible
to laugh from grief. Normally, Joy makes the heart beat faster,
so stimulating the midriff, which has a direct connection with
the muscles of the cheek and lips; laughter follows in consequence. In Grief, the contraction of the heart and the great con-
centration of blood and spirits about it, hinder the natural movement of the midriff; consequently the facial muscles are contracted, and the sufferer is seen to grin.[42] There is another cause
for this phenomenon, which arises when a man experiences the
desire for Revenge,

which causeth a / dilation of joy, entermedled with contraction of griefe: so a man that hath receaved a displeasure of his enimie, and assured how he may bee even with him, will laugh, though he have indignation at the displeasure, upon hope of requittance: whereof riseth a certaine joye mixed with griefe, that forceth out a Sardonian, bitter laughter . . .[43]

This recalls the description of Ferdinand when Bosola brings news of the discovery of the Duchess of Malfy's husband:

> The Lord Ferdinand laughes—
> Like a deadlie cannon
> That lightens ere it smoakes.[44]

The most powerful relief of the heart, however, was in speech, as Bacon says:

A principal fruit of friendship is the ease and discharge of the fulness and swellings of the heart, which passions of all kinds do cause and induce. We know diseases of stoppings and suffocation are the most dangerous in the body; and it is not much otherwise in the mind: you may take *sarza* to open the liver, steel to open the spleen, flowers of sulphur for the lungs, *castoreum* for the brain; but no receipt openeth the heart, but a tried friend, to whom you may impart griefs, joys, fears, hopes, suspicions, counsels, and whatsoever lieth upon the heart to oppress it, in a kind of civil shrift or confession.[45]

Thus when the news of the slaughter of his wife and children is brought to Macduff, he is urged to give his grief vent:

> Give sorrow words; the griefe that do's not speake,
> Whispers the O're-fraught heart, and bids it breake.[46]

The convention by which Elizabethan tragic heroes 'tear a passion to shreds' in burning utterance was not only good theatrical value; it was sound psychological theory. It is part of Hamlet's original distress that he must conceal his grief, suspicion and foreboding:

> It is not, nor it cannot come to good.
> But breake my heart, for I must hold my tongue.[47]

An honest man's passions would betray themselves in his appearance even if he did not disclose them in speech:

The heart of a man changeth his countenance, whether it be in good or evill: for in anger or feare we see men, eyther extreame pale, or

I

high-coloured; in melancholy or sadness, the eyes are heavy, in joy or pleasure, the motions of the eyes are lively and pleasant, according to the olde proverbe, *Cor gaudens exhilarat faciem*, a rejoycing heart maketh merry the face. And questionless wise men often, thorowe the windowes of the face, behold the secrets of the heart . . .[48]

Physiologically the reason for this was that the skin of the face was thinner than that of the rest of the body, and allowed the motions of the blood to be better seen:

> The signes of these Symptomes quickly shew themselves in the face: the heart, by reason of the thinnesse of the skinne in that part, as it were painting forth the notes of the affections.[49]

Donne's famous image in *The Second Anniversary* is a poetic transmutation of this:

> her pure, and eloquent blood
> Spoke in her cheekes, and so distinctly wrought,
> That one might almost say, her body thought . . .[50]

As Wright indicates, the most revealing organ was the eye. Davies of Hereford neatly expresses what was in fact a commonplace:

> The direct *Index* of the *Minde*, the *Eyes*
> Doth oft bewraie what *Reason* doth conceale:
> For wil yee, nil yee, we shal see thereby
> What's well, or ill, i'the *Mindes* commonweale.[51]

Shakespeare refers several times to the 'sympathy' between the eyes and the heart.[52] Wright points out that it is unfitting for inferiors to look their superiors in the eye, for they may thus reveal their own thoughts, or worse still surprise unworthy passions in their masters. The humble lowering of the eye before greatness provides Troilus with a simile for his confusion at the thought of Cressida's nearness:

> My heart beates thicker then a feavorous pulse,
> And all my powers doe their bestowing loose,
> Like vassalage at unawares encountring
> The eye of Majestie.[53]

The colour, size and shape of the eyes were of significance to the physiognomer.[54] Red, dry and fiery eyes, it is no surprise to learn, argued a stout, angry, wicked and shameless nature; black eyes were a sign of fearfulness and covetousness; blue, of a sharp piercing wit and courteous nature, and so on. Little eyes, according to some, indicated faint-heartedness, but Walkington says 'little eyes denote a large cheverill conscience'. Large eyes were a sign of gentleness and tractability (on the analogy of the ox); if they were trembling or quivering they revealed one very desirous of women. Large, protuberant eyes were a sign of foolishness: 'who open their eyes and extend them much, commonly be simple men, but of a good nature.' Very wide open eyes, staring fixedly, could also be a sign of impudence and incontinence in women. Long, narrow eyes indicated craft and deceit; hollow, deep-sunk eyes envy and malice. The movement of the eyes was also significant. A heavy eye indicated slowness and dullness of conceit, and was common in old or sick men, phlegmatics, and those suffering the passion of grief. A wandering eye showed vanity and untruth; a sharp, twinkling eye, malice and craft; frequent winking, fearfulness, 'because it argues a weaknesse of spirits, and a feeble disposition of the eyelids'. A rolling eye was a bad sign; it came from an abundance of hot spirits and indicated a hot and choleric complexion. In men it went with a quick but shallow wit and an incertain and impatient mind; in women with immodesty and wantonness. Malecasta, the Lady of Delight, displays this sign:

> She seemd a woman of great bountihed,
> And of rare beautie, saving that askaunce
> Her wanton eyes, ill signes of womanhed,
> Did roll too lightly, and too often glaunce,
> Without regard of grace, or comely amenaunce.[55]

A face that did not reveal the workings of the soul was the face of a villain. Thus, in the Third part of *Henry VI*, York rails at Queen Margaret:

> But that thy Face is Vizard-like, unchanging,
> Made impudent with use of evill deedes,
> I would assy, prowd Queene, to make thee blush.[56]

Concealment or dissimulation of passion were alike Hypocrisy, whose first inventor was Satan.[57] Shakespeare's villains are dissimulators. Iago is quite frank; Richard III impudently cynical in his advice to the young prince:

For when my outward Action doth demonstrate
The native act, and figure of my heart
In complement externe, 'tis not long after
But I will weare my heart upon my sleeve
For Dawes to pecke at; I am not what I am . . .

Sweet Prince, the untainted vertue of your yeers
Hath not yet div'd into the Worlds deceit:
No more can you distinguish of a man,
Then of his outward shew, which God he knowes,
Seldome or never jumpeth with the heart . . .[58]

Macbeth is not so accomplished a villain. At first his emotions clearly reveal themselves:

Your face, my *Thane*, is as a Booke, where men
May reade strange matters,

and here, as later before the banquet, Lady Macbeth has to urge him to disguise them:

Gentle my Lord, sleeke o're your rugged Lookes,
Be bright and Joviall among your guests to Night . . .

But by the end of the play he is so far advanced in villainy, or so lost in the horror into which he has plunged himself, that nothing has any effect on him:

The time ha's beene, my sences would have cool'd
To heare a Night-shrieke, and my Fell of haire
Would at a dismall treatise rowze, and stirre
As life were in't . . .[59]

Normally the passions of Shakespeare's characters are very visible to the beholder. Polixenes, for example, quickly sees the change in Leontes' attitude towards him:

The King hath on him such a countenance
As he had lost some Province, and a Region
Lov'd, as he loves himselfe: even now I met him
With customarie complement, when hee
Wafting his eyes to th'contrary, speedes from me, and
So leaves me, to consider what is breeding,
That changes thus his Manners.[60]

It is in fact remarkable with what freedom Shakespeare and his contemporaries describe the display of emotion by characters who are actually on the stage and in full view of the audience. Thus when Hubert brings the news of Arthur's death to King John, the Earls of Pembroke and Salisbury comment:

> *Pem.* This is the man should do the bloody deed:
> He shew'd his warrant to a friend of mine,
> The image of a wicked heynous fault
> Lives in his eye: that close aspect of his,
> Does shew the mood of a much troubled brest,
> And I do fearefully beleeve 'tis done,
> What we so fear'd he had a charge to do.
> *Sal.* The colour of the King doth come, and go
> Betweene his purpose and his conscience,
> Like Heralds 'twixt two dreadfull battailes set:
> His passion is so ripe, it needs must break.[61]

In these scenes, which often cause difficulty on the modern stage, we have probably to allow a certain amount for convention. Very possibly the Elizabethan audience demanded no more than a reasonable congruity between the actor's appearance and the signs of emotion which he was described as displaying. The existence of accepted gestures as symbols of different passions would make the actor's task easier.[62] We have nevertheless the very striking case of the First Player in *Hamlet*. The description given of his simulated passion is unequivocal:

> Is it not monstrous that this Player heere,
> But in a Fixion, in a dreame of Passion,
> Could force his soule so to his whole conceit,
> That from her working, all his visage wanned;
> Teares in his eyes, distraction in's Aspect,
> A broken voyce, and his whole Function suiting
> With Formes, to his conceit?[63]

The whole point here is that the Player, who has no real cause for passion, can display it, while Hamlet, who has a real cause, can not; it would be largely lost if the Player did not in fact reproduce the most violent signs of outward passion. It may be that since it was considered natural and wholesome for passion to be expressed freely in everyday life, the actor was less inhibited than he tends to be in our more reticent age.

The general belief that 'true plaine hearts doe in the faces rest'[64] resulted in trust in appearance as a guide to character, which was codified in the doctrines of Physiognomy. This pseudo-science, like its sisters Chiromancy, Astrology and Oneiromancy, does not admit of easy summary. It was based on a combination of principles, if principles they can be called. The ultimate basis was observation of human types, observation organized by the popular mind into tradition. This produced such mnemonic rhymes as this, quoted by Wright, which sums up the nature of women:

> Faire and foolish, little and lowde,
> Long and lazie, blacke and prowde:
> Fatte, and merrie, leane, and sadde:
> Pale, and pettish; red and badde.[65]

Nearly allied to this was the attempt to discern the characters of men from their resemblance to different animals. We still employ this method ourselves when we describe a man as 'rabbit-chinned' or 'fishy-eyed', and expect him to display the lack of pugnacity or the cold-bloodedness which we associate with these animals. A more sophisticated approach lay through the physical characteristics of the different temperatures or complexions. These have perhaps already been sufficiently described, but we may continue the theme of feminine types by quoting from Marston's *The Fawn*. Hercules, the flatterer, is discoursing on the favourite theme of the amorous Nymphado:

> Nay, for every humour of a man in that hour, to have a several mistress to entertain him; as if he were saturnine, or melancholy, to have a black-haired, palefaced, sallow, thinking mistress to clip him: if jovial and merry, a sanguine, light-tripping, singing—indeed a mistress that would dance a coranto as she goes to embrace him: if choleric, impatient, or ireful, to have a mistress with red hair, little ferret eyes, a lean cheek and a sharp nose to entertain him.[66]

This is the kind of judgement which Caesar employs on Cassius. The 'lean and hungry look' would indicate the malcontent choleric, and also the student who thinks too much.[67] Fat men would be either sanguines or phlegmatics, types not likely to wish to subvert Authority.

Another guide to the temperature of the body was the temperature of the hand:

> for the veines, beeing derived from the Liver . . . and being united, and meeting in the Hand; they are the cause of that Mutuall and Reciprocall sympathy that there is betweene those two parts. And so by consequent, the Temperature of the Liver will appeare more evidently in the Hand, then in many other of the parts of the Body.[68]

Thus it was that hot, moist palms were taken as a sign of a wanton, sanguine disposition.[69] The rest of the body also revealed 'temperature', though less immediately than the hand. The bodies of melancholiacs were cold and dry to the touch; those of phlegmatics, cold and clammy. Physical signs could also be held to reveal the presence of a master-passion. Because the hair stood on end in fear, for example, a man whose hair was naturally upstanding was of a fearful nature. Similarly red eyes argued an angry nature. Finally among these theoretical grounds of physiognomy came reference to the physical characteristics associated with the influence of the planets or astrological signs. These might be very specific, descending even to small marks on the body. Thus the pseudonymous Dr. Arcandam notes of a man born under the 'head of Aries' that he 'shall also have upon his left foote a syne or marke, and the like upon the left elbow'.[70]

On this mixed basis was built up a considerable body of rules, with rather less confusion and inconsistency than might have been expected. Fortunately we do not have to investigate many of the finer points. A practising dramatist, especially in the Elizabethan theatre, could not pay attention to minutiae of appearance—certainly not, for instance, to the placing of moles. To a large extent he would have to take his actors as he found them, although we can be certain that the actors could employ wigs and beards, and also some make-up, to change their appearance. We may consider, then, complexion (in our sense), and the colour and nature of the hair as guides to character. Movement and gesture also would be easy for an actor to imitate, and these too may be considered.

A red face was (naturally) a sign of wrathful man or a drunkard, if it were very red or fiery; a ruddy or less red complexion indicated a mischievous man or one 'endued with variable

manners'. A mixture of red and white in the face showed a stout
and strong person, but a pale complexion was an ill sign:

> *Diogenes* seeing a pale wan-faced young Man, said he was either in
> love, or was malicious: For envious persons are vexed with the good
> successe of other men, wax lean, and their marrow and bones corrupt
> within them.[71]

A pale countenance also hinted at a fearful disposition. A wan,
leaden or yellowish colour showed a vicious and luxurious
nature, but a swarthy or brown complexion was a sign of good
wit and honest manners. A sallow skin showed one who talked
too much and was stupid. As Hill points out, however, all these
signs had to be interpreted with regard to the climate, which
might alter the complexion without reference to the disposition.[72]
   The colour of the hair was also affected by climate. In general,
however, red hair—'Judas-colour'—was a sign of deceivers,
choleric men and such as were full of wrath. White or very fair
hair indicated the phlegmatic temperament and men with
'wanton manners and conditions'. Black hair, if it were curled
and crisp, was a sign of great heat, and therefore of a warlike and
lecherous nature; if it was lank and straight, it indicated fearfulness and covetousness. Golden or honey-coloured hair showed a
medium-cold temperature, and a nature proud, haughty and
vainglorious. The most favourable colour was chestnut, which
went with a well-balanced temperament and a nature upright,
just and well-beloved of men. Hair was an excrement, and its
quantity depended on the amount of vital heat and moisture in
the body. It appears that the thickness of the individual hairs
corresponded to the amount of moisture in the body, and the
profusion of hair to the heat.[73] The amount of curl in the hair
also depended on heat. Thus smooth, thick, straight hair indicated a cold and moist temperature, and therefore went with
meekness and cowardice. Scanty hair also indicated lack of heat.
For that reason, women were chary of giving their affection to
men with little beard:

> not so much, for that they are commonly cold and impotent, as that,
> so much resembling Eunuches, they are for the most part inclined
> to baseness, cruelty and deceitfulnesse.[74]

Great hairiness, on the other hand, indicated a very hot temperament, particularly on the chest, where it showed great hotness of heart, and so strength and courage. There were cases of very valiant men whose hearts, at their death, were found to be covered with hair.[75]

Gesture also reflected temperature. Heavy, slow movements obviously corresponded to a phlegmatic or melancholic temperament: quick, light movements to a more fiery and volatile disposition. This must have been taken into account by the actor and the orator in their 'action'—that is, the gestures with which they accompanied their speech. Hill gives us two vivid pictures of different types of 'action': first, the flatterer:

> Such which shrugge to and fro with the body, and rubbing themselves, and if these properly be eloquent, are noted mightie flatterers, and dissemblers: applyed to the Spaniell; the which partly for feare, and partly for reliefe at his masters handes, doth so shrugge togither, and fleere or fawne on his master.[76]

The dog, of course, is a favourite symbol with Shakespeare (and others) for the fawner and lick-spittle. Hill also describes the villain meditating his villainy:

> Such which sometimes looke to the earth, with a clowdie and frowning foreheade, and the upper eye-liddes drawne togither, and that the eyes sometimes turne upwarde, with a bearing upright of the heade: are noted to be wholly occupied in wicked devises and thoughtes.[77]

Perhaps it was this which provoked Hamlet's

> Pox, leave thy damnable Faces; and begin![78]

Gait was a powerful sign of character. Thus Arcandam notes:

> when the man goeth lightly having al his body upright, it is a signe that hee will take in hand some enterprise, and by and by doe some great thing. But if a man goe swiftly with his eyes looking downward and goe altogether crooked, it is a signe of a niggard, fearful and subtile.[79]

This may give us some idea of how the Elizabethan actor would make his entrance in the appropriate circumstances. Hill describes the ponderous gait which the gull affecting melancholy would adopt:

If any hath a curious slowness of pace (that sometimes staying) turneth the head, and looketh about him; doth bewray such a person, to be high minded.[80]

He also describes a totally different manner of walking:

Such which go with a leaping or dauncing pase, and bearing out the buttock, and with the countenance borne upright, are noted to be Cyneds and womanly persons.[81]

This recalls Henry IV's scornful description of Richard II:

The skipping King hee ambled up and downe.[82]

Finally, Lemnius, in describing the gait proper to the perfect complexion, incidentally gives us an indication of stage habit:

The parte and state of the body bolt uprighte, the gate in going framed to comelynes, not nycely affected nor curiously counterfaicted, as it were Players and disguised Masquers, who by a kinde of upstarte and stately gate, hopeth the rather to winne credite, estimation and authority, and to be made more accompte of, among the common people.[83]

Something should perhaps also be said of voice as a guide to character, although not as much attention seems to have been paid to this as might have been expected. A melodious voice was a sign of a harmonious disposition, and a harsh and discordant voice of an evil and cruel nature. A feeble voice was a sign of weakness and cowardice:

the force of the voice followeth the wideness of the veines, and the multitude of spirits: al which things / come of heat. . . . A weak voice betokeneth narrow arteries and want of spirit, which things come of cold.[84]

Conversely,

such a person which hath a grosse, high, and sounding voyce, is reported to be eloquent, bold, fierce and valiant in armes . . .[85]

To speak now loud, now low and imperfectly was a sign of a fearful nature and was common in women. To speak softly showed a gentle and simple nature, on the analogy of the sheep. A voice slow but with a 'big sound' indicated a man quiet, tractable, merry, and just. A shrill voice was of course a sign of anger, while to speak very loudly was the mark of a frantic man and a glutton.[86]

It was generally agreed that the rules of physiognomy were not implicitly to be relied on; they did not necessarily discover the passions, but 'only for the most part, and probably'.[87] Duncan comments sadly on the defection of Cawdor:

> There's no Art,
> To find the Mindes construction in the Face:
> He was a Gentleman, on whom I built
> An absolute trust.[88]

Nevertheless it seemed reasonable to suppose that in general terms the appearance of the body should be a guide to the nature of the soul. Deformity at least should be good ground for suspicion. Lemnius explains:

> For where there is an errour about some principal part, there the mind partakes of some inconvenience, and cannot perfectly perform her offices. So that they that are deformed with a bunch-back, so it be a natural Infirmity, and not accidental, nor come by fall or blow, are commonly wicked and malitious, because the deprivation is communicated to the heart, that is the fountain and beginning of life.[89]

Richard III's attitude to his own deformity is a blend of fatalism and sardonic humour; since Nature has spoiled him as a man, he seems to say, there is nothing for him to do but to fulfil the promise of his appearance and play the villain.[90] The explanation which Lemnius offers for the correlation between deformity and evil—that the soul cannot express her full nature in a deformed body—is rather 'modern' and rationalistic. Spenser follows the more traditional view that the immortal soul impresses her nature upon her fleshly dwelling-place:

> Which powre retaining still or more or less,
> When she in fleshly seede is eft enraced,
> Through every part she doth the same impresse,
> According as the heavens have her graced,
> And frames her house, in which she will be placed
> Fit for herself, adorning it with spoyle
> Of th'heavenly riches which she robd erewhile.[91]

Thus the more virtuous the soul, the more beautiful the body, and conversely. Beauty displayed itself chiefly in the face:

> There is nothing more beautifull in man than his soule; and in the body of man than his visage, which is as it were the soule abreviated.
> . . . The Beauty of the body, especially the visage, should in all reason demonstrate and witnesse the beauty of the soule . . . for ther is no-thing that hath a truer resemblance than the conformity and relation of the body to the spirit.[92]

Nevertheless, it could not be maintained that all ugly people were wicked. The neo-Platonic answer to this objection was that sometimes the stubborn material of the body resisted the shaping spirit:

> it is a thing certaine, that Beautie proceedeth from forme, and deformitie from matter; the which, as it is of his owne proper nature unformall, so al deformitie hath from it derivation: For matter resisteth Ideall reason, so that in her shee cannot produce the perfect forme shee intendeth . . .[93]

There remained the still more difficult question of the beautiful wicked person, the hypocrite or 'white devil'. Spenser and his fellow neo-Platonists failed to provide a convincing solution to this problem. Their opponents seized on this point, and maintained on their side that beauty in man was a sign of a cold, and therefore feeble and possibly wicked nature,[94] while in women:

> there is alwaies a great combat betwixt chastitie and beauty, so that we seldome see faire women to be honest matrons: the reason is, because they preferre the phantasticall pleasure of their bodily senses, before the true and right noble vertues of the mind. Such (as the *Spaniard* saith) are like an apple, which is faire without and rotten within . . .[95]

Majority popular opinion was probably with the neo-Platonists, with reservations. It was in any case clear that there was no absolute standard of Beauty; it lay in the eye of the beholder:

> for the Conditions that are required by the Naturalists in an Absolute Beauty, are so many, as that there cannot be found in the whole world a person so accomplished with all the necessary circumstances of Beauty, but that each part will afford a sufficient matter for a Criticall eye to finde fault with. . . Whence we may conclude, that the rarest and most excellent Beauties that are, are not such indeed,

as they seeme to be: but onely appeare to be so, through the sole defect of the beholders, and through the weakness of their Eyes.[96]

The whole question of the relation of Beauty to goodness was of great importance because of Beauty's power to distress the soul by awakening the violent passion of Love. This was Adam's one weakness:

> here passion first I felt
> Commotion strange, in all enjoyments else
> Superior and unmov'd, here onely weake
> Against the charm of Beauties powerful glance.[97]

There was a natural inclination in Man towards what Coeffeteau calls 'beauty and bounty' (that is, goodness).[98] But lovers were in no fit condition to judge of either. Ferrand discourses vigorously on the tendency of lovers to 'see Helen's beauty in a brow of Egypt':

> For doe we not oftimes see young spruce gallants enamoured with some old, crooked, deformed *Hecuba*, with a furroughed forehead, long hairy eye-browes, bleare eyes, long hanging eares, a saddle nose, thick blabber lipps, black stinking teeth with a long terrible chin hanging downe to her girdle: which yet they will sweare is a second *Helen*, whose beauty shines most resplendently in those lovely wrinkles . . .[99]

Lovers were equally liable to see virtue where it in fact did not exist. They were, in fact, particularly likely to fall into the errors of Opinion, judging only by external appearance, and not always correctly by that. They were consequently only too liable to error, and to sudden changes of heart. This is Cressida's fault, as she says herself:

> *Troylus* farewell; one eye yet lookes on thee;
> But with my heart, the other eye, doth see,
> Ah poore our sexe; this fault in us I finde:
> The errour of our eye, directs our minde.
> What errour leads, must erre: O then conclude,
> Mindes swai'd by eyes, are full of turpitude.[100]

It was usual to distinguish three kinds of Love, corresponding to the three orders of living beings—plants, animals, men—and to the three powers of the Soul. Natural Love was a product of Natural Appetite; it accounted for the affinities which were observed between certain plants and trees. Sensible Love was the love of beasts; it was a compound of desire, the philoprogenitive instinct, attraction of like to like, and habit. Rational Love was the love of men, and was akin to the love of Angels and of God.[101] This love might have three objects, which Burton lists as Profit, Pleasure and Honesty.[102] Love for Profit was the love a poor man displayed to a rich, or a courtier to a great man; it was fallacious and soon fading. Love for pleasure was akin to Sensible Love, and was violent, self-deluding, and unstable. Love for Honesty was love of intellectual virtue, and took the higher form of Friendship. Friendship was a branch of Justice, since it was only truly bestowed where it was deserved, and was also, since it contained the desire to please and reward, related to the supreme Christian virtue of Charity. The Love of God was a kind of Divine Friendship, since it bestowed grace on those who loved Him and deserved well of His hands.

Some maintained that it was impossible for true love or friendship to exist between man and woman. For one thing, it almost unavoidably became corrupted by 'beastly' appetite. Again, friendship could only exist between equals, and Woman was not the equal of man. It could even be claimed that Woman had no soul, or at best only an imperfect soul, and was therefore incapable of loving intellectual things. Nearly all Coeffeteau's examples of Love are of passionate, idealized friendship between men. This view was on the whole suspect in England, for it was felt to tend towards a vice more suitable to the Italian than to the honest Englishman. Renaissance England was not ignorant of homosexuality and other sexual deviations nor mealy-mouthed in speaking of them. Marston's *Scourge of Villainie* will suffice to support both these assertions. They were regarded, however, as unnatural sins and the psychologist did not feel called on to pay them much attention. Burton, for example, cites various perversions as example of the tyranny of Love, but declares himself 'unwilling to inquire any longer into such evils'.[103] This concept of Love was therefore not common in this country, but its influence can be seen in a high regard for friendship—in, for example, the relations between Brutus and Cassius, Hamlet and Horatio, or Melantius and Amintor in *The Maid's Tragedy*.[104] It is reflected also in the use of the language of Love between men, most notably in Shakespeare's Sonnets.[105]

The opposite pole to this theory of Love was the code of
Courtly Love, as modified by neo-Platonism. This was far easier
to accept, but strictly judged it, too, was a heresy. The love of
beauty in women might be a step on the road to a love of God,
but it was only too easy to fall into the simple error of identifying
Beauty with Virtue. Moreover it could not be right for Man, the
superior animal, to bow down to his natural inferior and submit
his judgement to hers: that was how Adam fell. The beauty of
woman might well attract:

> For, though minde be the heaven, where love doth sit,
> Beauty a convenient type may be to figure it;[106]

but true Love must see beyond, to 'the inward beauty of her
lively spright'.[107] Charron explains that 'the marriage of true
minds' was something finer than friendship or pure passion:

> The third kind of friendship in regard of the persons is mixed, and
> . . . is, or it should be more strong; this is matrimoniall of married
> couples, which holdeth of love or friendship in a straight line, because
> of the superioritie of the wife: and of collateral friendship, being
> both of them companions joyned together by equall bands.[108]

Nevertheless it was hard, in the grip of an overmastering
passion, to be sure that the Judgement had rightly perceived the
truth. The two desired qualities in the beloved were Beauty and
Virtue; the presence of one might lead the lover to infer the
presence of the other. This might not matter when admiration
for her virtue led the lover to credit his beloved with beauty; but
the obverse was of great danger, as Claudio realizes:

> O *Hero*! What a *Hero* hadst thou beene
> If half thy outward graces had been placed
> About thy thoughts and counsailes of thy heart?
> But fare thee well, most foule, most faire, farewell
> Thou pure impiety, and impious puritie,
> For thee Ile lock up all the gates of Love,
> And on my eie-lids shall Conjecture hang,
> To turne all beauty into thoughts of harme,
> And never more shall it be gracious.[109]

The discovery of Cressida's infidelity brings Troilus face to
face with this conflict between appearance and reality, a conflict

which seems irreconcilable. Othello, more the man of action, puts into practice the principle which Charron enunciates:

> they that belie their owne physiognomie, are rather to be punisht than others, because they falsifie and betray that good promise that Nature hath planted in their front, and deceive the world.[110]

Thus he can justify his murder as almost a ritual purification, and see himself as removing from the world the greatest of stumbling-blocks, a beautiful evil:

> Yet she must dye, else shee'l betray more men.[111]

Beauty was a powerful, but possibly a fallacious guide to Virtue, and when the whole theory of man's nature was so bound up with the ideas of Harmony, Beauty, Order and Balance it could not be other than tragic to find that the system could contain flaws.

Chapter Six

CONCLUSION

THE errors and weaknesses of Renaissance psychology are evident. The very fact that it was so closely allied to physiological theory, which was in one way its greatest asset, was also its greatest source of danger. It could not hope to survive the development of a more accurate and scientific knowledge of the body, and even by the time that Shakespeare was writing its foundations had been undermined. The seventeenth century saw it collapse; not suddenly or dramatically, but quietly and apparently without disturbance. Those parts of the theory which were untenable were relinquished; those not immediately affected were retained. Hobbes, for example, whose attitude to mental processes was in many respects radically different from that of a Renaissance writer, still derives the Passions from the twin powers of Appetite and Aversion, as Aquinas had done, and there are many points of resemblance, even of verbal similarity, between Pope's *Essay on Man* and Sir John Davies' *Nosce Teipsum*. Elements of the system persist throughout the eighteenth century. To take a trivial example: Narcissa's aunt, in the 39th chapter of *Roderick Random*, reproduces one of the classical delusions of the melancholiac, and is cured by one of the classic remedies. (The popularity of *The Anatomy of Melancholy* among the curious probably helped to keep the system alive longer.) We ourselves retain traces of the psychology of Shakespeare's day in our everyday speech. We talk quite naturally of a happy temperament, or a bad temper; of a jovial or saturnine disposition; of animal spirits or a heart moved by passion. Although such expressions are almost completely fossilized, there are feeble stirrings of life still left in them.

In the seventeenth century, however, the essential unity of the Renaissance system was disrupted. Psychology was divided into three spheres: that of the Physician, that of the Philosopher, and

K

that of the Theologian. The first was concerned with the body and bodily illnesses without inquiring too far into the relations between physical and mental health. The second devoted his attention to the problems of perception and cognition, sensation and association, and on his side ignored the physical basis of mind. Questions of the ultimate nature and value of human experience were left to the theologian. In this disruption the science of psychology proper made little or no advance, and not until, in the second half of the nineteenth century, psychology was recognized as a subject in its own right and some reunion was effected between psychology and physiology were any great steps taken forward. To some extent, however, the value of these advances has been offset by the difficulty which the layman experiences in understanding them, and in this the Renaissance has the advantage of us.

The Renaissance psychologist could claim to provide a comprehensive system understandable, perhaps not by all, but by all educated men. This merit was general to all science, and the unity of the psychological system was part of the greater unity of the whole Renaissance view of the Universe. The opinions offered to Shakespeare of the nature of Man and of the Universe were not accurate or scientific, sometimes not even common-sensible, but they could at least claim the virtue of being satisfying. If Shakespeare was prepared to accept certain axioms and overlook certain difficulties he was provided with a neat, integrated and orderly account of human existence which was reasonably consistent with everyday experience and reasonably plausible in its account of matters beyond human ken. There can be no doubt that Shakespeare was so prepared; there is little evidence in him of a dissatisfaction with the world-view offered by his age. The system, apart from the comfort it could give to the lonely human soul, had certain advantages to offer the poet. Since it employed analogy as a principal mode of inquiry and explanation, it provided a ready-made stock of metaphors and similes. It was a poetic universe, in that all its parts were related to each other; it was full of parallels, correspondences and symbols. Shakespeare might be thought to be the last poet to stand in need of such assistance, but in fact he does often make use of it—not consciously, perhaps, but because such was the mental habit of his time. When Falstaff, to take a simple example, greets the newly crowned Henry V with the words, 'My King, My Jove, I speak to thee, my Heart!'[1] he is doing more than string together three titles of honour and affection. Jupiter was chief of the planets as the heart was the principal organ of the body, and the King is rightly compared to both. Many other examples of this kind of thinking can be found in Shakespeare: there are several in the quotations included in this book. When we turn to the second- or third-rate Elizabethan poets we are no doubt right in finding much of their imagery derivative, commonplace, and merely ornamental, but we should remember that what to us may be only dead metaphor was to them a direct and vivid expression of their own knowledge of the Universe.

In a more limited sphere, we should naturally tend to assume that Renaissance psychological theory would have little to teach Shakespeare of human nature. Certainly it could have been no substitute for genuine and keenly-felt experience, but it must have entered into the organization and understanding of that experience. Shakespeare, we feel, would have manifested a profound understanding of human nature in any age; since he was an Elizabethan he expressed it in Elizabethan terms. If we demand of one of his characters that they should conform to *our* psychological ideas we are exceeding our just rights; they are true to the psychology of their own day. It may, however, be as well to repeat a warning against the assumption that Shakespeare's characters—or those of any other Elizabethan or Jacobean dramatist—are rigidly bound to the framework of contemporary psychological theory. Objections have rightly been made to a literal interpretation of dramatic figures or poetic expressions in terms of the doctrines outlined in this book.[2] Very often writers disregarded the theorists; sometimes they misunderstood them; frequently they misapplied technical terminology. As always, the critic must use the material supplied by the scholar with discretion. In any case it would be superficial to suggest that the psychological theorists were agreed at all points. There was a considerable amount of disagreement on matter of detail, and even on some matters of major importance.[3] Nevertheless, there was a substantially agreed body of opinion ready for Shakespeare if he wished to consult it. That he ever formally did so we may doubt. It is not easy to imagine Shakespeare 'reading up' the characteristics of melancholy in Bright and Du Laurens before he began writing *Hamlet*. On the other hand, it is probably equally false to believe (as some critics apparently do) that Shakespeare only read those contemporary works from which he intended to take the plots of his plays. It is hardly too much to credit him with taking a general interest in the thought of his day. It is in fact easier to illustrate contemporary psychology from Shakespeare than from any of his contemporaries, not excepting Ben Jonson. That he was familiar with the general outline of Renaissance psychology, and with some at least of its details, should have been made obvious by this book.

The contemporary ideas of Man had something to offer Shakespeare also as a philosophical writer. It came naturally to him, for example, to see cosmic parallels to the sin and madness of a tragic hero; his age was accustomed to that manner of thought. When the relationship between Man and the Universe was so close, a story of human frailty and suffering easily assumed philosophical and religious significance. Again, the Elizabethan and Jacobean dramatists—and Shakespeare among them—have sometimes been accused of representing violence and passion on the stage for their own sake. Of this they were no doubt sometimes guilty, but a passionate hero to them was not merely a powerful dramatic spectacle, but a vivid example of the dangers which beset the human soul. Dr. Johnson accused Shakespeare of lacking a consistent moral purpose, and, in the sense in which Johnson intended the charge, it must be admitted to be true. It is difficult to prove that Shakespeare deliberately wrote to point a moral in any of his plays, although moral questions may be incidentally discussed in them. But the universe in which Shakespeare lived and in which his plays are set was a moral universe. The Providence and Wisdom of God brooded over it, and controlled its slightest events. If we attempt to construct a moral or philosophical system on the basis of Shakespeare's plays alone we are apt to find outselves involved in ambiguities and unwarranted assumptions. If we set the plays in the context of the thought of their time, what is implicit in them becomes more plain. Much time has been spent in discussing the nature of Shakespeare's 'Tragic World'. If we look at the tragedies in the light of contemporary psychological theory we can see that in all except *Hamlet* and *Julius Caesar* evil enters the mind of the hero in the shape of a passion; the passion grows until it over-

comes the Reason; in consequence the hero sins, or at least be-
haves irrationally; finally retribution overtakes his sin. It is a
perfect formula for Tragedy.[4] In this sense the tragedies (and
the other plays) are moral and philosophical, because they por-
tray the mind of Man.

There is always a danger when we turn back to recover the
thought of the past that we may be seized by an irrational fondness for what has passed away. None of us would care to live in
the Elizabethan world, or would willingly entrust our illnesses
to an Elizabethan doctor. Not all his errors were so senseless as
they may at first sight appear, and many of his colleagues were
among the most enlightened men of the day, both as scientists
and as humanitarians. Nevertheless, his knowledge was very
limited; his methods crude; and his cures (we cannot but feel)
largely fortuitous. When he turned his attention to the mind and
became a psychologist we have less certain grounds for criticiz-
ing him, since our own knowledge of the mind is so tentative
and hypothetical. If his concepts were false, many of them have
survived in the popular mind until the present day. We may
perhaps be surprised at the acuteness of some of his observations
while rejecting as outworn the framework in which he placed
them. When he related his theories to the world surrounding
him, and became a moralist and a philosopher, we can at least
admire the thoughtfulness and the sense of responsibility which
he displays. Without antiquarian fondness we may respect a
system which made a serious attempt to deal with the central
problems of human existence.

NOTES

Chapter One

INTRODUCTION

Page 14

1. *Epistle* I, ll. 233–46 (ed. Mack, pp. 44–5). The most exhaustive study of the Great Chain is A. O. Lovejoy, *The Great Chain of Being*. See also E. M. W. Tillyard, *The Elizabethan World Picture*, esp. pp. 22–33.

2. *Nosce Teipsum*, p. 38.

Page 15

3. Primaudaye, *The French Academy*, tr. Bowes *et al.* (1618), pp. 423–4.

4. *Paradise Lost*, Bk. V, ll. 404 ff.

5. *Essay on Man*, Epistle II, l. 8 (ed. Mack, p. 55).

6. *To Sir Edward Herbert*, ll. 1–18. (*Poetical Works*, ed. Grierson, Vol. I, pp. 193–4.)

Page 16

7. Barckley, *A Discourse of the Felicitie of Man*, pp. 5–6.

8. *Paradise Lost*, IX, 1121–31.

Page 17

9. E.g. Nashe in *Pierce Pennilesse* (*Works*, ed. McKerrow, Vol. I, pp. 207–8). Cf. *Canterbury Tales*, Group H, ll. 44–5 and edd. notes.

10. *Comus*, ll. 527–30. Comus's 'baneful cup' is the same as that proffered to Sir Guyon by Excess in *The Faerie Queene*, Bk. II, Canto XII, stanza lvi. Cf. also *Othello*, II, iii, 268–9, 297–9, 314–15.

11. *Holy Observations*, ch. 80. (*Works*, 1625, p. 148.) Cf. *Canterbury Tales*, C 492–7 (*The Pardoner's Tale*).

Page 19

12. *Timon*, IV, iii, 176–95.

13. Sonnet CXXIX, ll. 1–4.

14. Nashe, *Christ's Teares over Jerusalem* (McKerrow II, pp. 112–13).

Page 20

15. *Lear*, III, iv, 97–9. Cf. *Cymbeline*, III, iii, 39–41, where Arviragus complains that he and his brothers have not been given the education which would permit them to develop their reason:

> We have seen nothing:
> We are beastly: subtle as the Fox for prey,
> Like warlike as the Wolfe, for what we eate.

Elsewhere Shakespeare speaks of 'the brutish sting' of sensuality (*As You Like It*, II, vii, 66); 'Brutish wrath' (*Richard III*, II, i, 118); and 'Beastly fury' (*Timon*, III, v. 72).

16. *Faerie Queene*, II, xi, v ff.

17. *Troilus*, I, iii, 119–24.

18. *Canterbury Tales*, I, 259–64. 'Sensualitee' =the lower faculties of man, which are concerned with the senses.

19. Romei, *The Courtier's Academy*, p. 17.

Page 21

20. Crooke, *Microcosmographia*, pp. 6–8.

Page 22

21. Forset, *A comparative Discourse of the Bodies natural and politique*, sig. iii r°. Shakespeare has a celebrated passage on the similitude of the bees in *Henry V*, I, ii, 183–204. The metaphor of 'the ship of state' is still familiar to us.

22. *Coriolanus*, I, i, 95 ff.

Page 23

23. *Julius Caesar*, II, i, 63–8.

24. *John*, IV, ii, 245–8.

25. *2 Henry IV*, V, ii, 129–37.

Page 24

26. *Tamburlaine*, Part I, II, i (ed. Brooke, ll. 465–70); *Anthony and Cleopatra*, V, ii, 79–81 (last line emended).

27. *Paradise Lost*, II, 890 ff.

28. *Paradise Lost*, III, 713.

29. See: *Faerie Queene*, VII, vii, xxv, and cf. Fletcher, *The Purple Island*, Canto I, stanza 42. No two elements possessed the same primary quality to the same degree. Thus both Air and Fire possessed the quality of Heat, but Air was less hot than fire because its other quality of moisture tempered its heat. Fire was primarily hot and secondarily dry; Air was primarily wet and secondarily hot; Water was primarily cold and

secondarily wet; Earth was primarily dry and secondarily cold. (See Jones, *The Bathes of Bathes Ayde*, f. 24 r°.)

30. Paré, *Works*, p. 6.

Page 25

31. Davies, *Orchestra*, st. 17–18. Cf. Spenser: *Hymne to Love*, ll. 78–91. It is significant that the ambitious and unnatural Tamburlaine, in a celebrated passage (*Tamburlaine*, Pt. I, ll. 869–71) refers the elements back to their original condition of chaos and makes them symbols of conflict. Implicit in this passage is the idea that all the elements aspire to the state of fire, which is the purest and most noble of them; this is particularly appropriate to Tamburlaine's arrogant, 'fiery' nature.

32. Elyot, *The Governor*, ed. Watson, pp. 28, 85 ff. For Castiglione's views, see *The Courtier*, tr. Hoby (ed. Henderson), pp. 75 ff.

33. *Merchant of Venice*, V, i, 83–5. Cf. Kyd, *The Spanish Tragedie*, (ed. Boas) III, xii, 169–72.

Page 26

34. Hooker, *Ecclesiastical Polity*, Bk. I, ch. 9 (ed. 1611, p. 23).

35. *Nosce Teipsum*, p. 2.

Page 27

36. *Anatomy*, Part I, section i, Member I, subsection i (ed. Shilleto, Vol. I, pp. 149–50).

37. *Nosce Teipsum*, p. 8. See D. C. Allen, *The Degeneration of Man and Renaissance Pessimism* (Stud. Phil., XXXII (1938), pp. 202–27.)

Chapter Two

THE SOUL

Page 29

1. *Anatomy*, I, i, II, v. (Shilleto I, p. 177.)

2. *Nosce Teipsum*, p. 11.

Page 30

3. Lemnius, *The Secret Miracles of Nature*, p. 40.

4. *Twelfth Night*, IV, ii, 57–8. Cf. Donne, *First Anniversarie*, ll. 451–3. (Grierson, I, pp. 244–5.)

5. *Nosce Teipsum*, p. 12. Cf. Aristotle, *De Anima*, Bk. II, ch. 1;

Aquinas, *Summa Theologica*, Pt. I, Question lxxv, Article 5. Davies gives an account of other views of the soul in *Nosce Teipsum*, pp. 10–11 (ultimately based on Aristotle, *De Anima*, I, 2).

Page 31

6. *Hymne to Beautie.* ll 132–3.

7. Romei, p. 27. The ultimate source is Plato, *Phaedo*, st. 86. Cf. *Hamlet*, III, i, 163–6.

8. *Anatomy*, I, i, II, v. (Shilleto, I, p. 177.)

9. Bartolomeus Anglicanus, *De proprietatibus Rerum*, ed. Stephen Bateman (1582), f. 14 rᵒ. Cf. *Lear*, I, i, 72–4. 'The Philosopher' is of course Aristotle; the reference is to *De Anima*, II, 3.

Page 32

10. *Twelfth Night*, II, iii, 59–60.

11. Aristotle, *De Anima*, II, 3; Aquinas, *Summa Theologica*, I, lxxvi, 3.

12. *Faerie Queene*, II, ix, xxii. 'Proportioned equally by seven and nine' may refer to the seven planets and the nine spheres: or 'seven' may refer to the combination of the four elements and the three spirits or souls, and 'nine' to the nine orders of angels in the celestial hierarchy. For other explanations, see *The Variorum Spenser*, Appendix xi to Book II.

13. See Aristotle, *De Anima*, II, 12. For the physical aspects of sensation, see below, p. 56.

Page 33

14. E.g., *Measure for Measure*, V, i, 141; Sonnet CXLI, l. 6.

15. Essay *Of Boldness* (Works, ed. Spedding *et al.*, VI, pp. 401–2).

16. *Coriolanus*, III, ii, 73–7. Wright, in *The Passions of the Mind in General* (p. 156), notes the importance of what we might call 'visual aids' in oratory; we might compare Anthony's use of Caesar's cloak and will in his speech in the Forum (*Julius Caesar*, III, ii, 136 ff., 177 ff.) Wright also (op. cit., p. 172 ff.) speaks of the moving effect of the sight of passion in others: cf. *Julius Caesar*, III, i, 282–5, where Anthony weeps at the sight of the servant's tears. For this reason it was important for the orator to be able to simulate passion.

17. *The Ecstasie*, ll. 7–8. (Grierson, I, p. 51.) Cf. Crooke, pp. 666 ff.

Page 34

18. Cornelius Agrippa, *Three Books of Occult Philosophy*, tr. Freak, p. 101. Cf. Bacon, *Of Envy* (Spedding, VI, pp. 392–3), and see L. Thorndike, *A History of Magic and Experimental Science*, Vol. V, pp. 475–6, 486–7.

19. Coeffeteau, *The Table of Humane Passions*, tr. Grimestone, p. 87. Cf. Ferrand, *Erotomania*, tr. Chilmead, pp. 68–70.

20. III, i, 88–95. (Text from the edition of 1617.) The most celebrated instance of a lover pierced through the eye is Palamon in *The Knight's Tale* (*Canterbury Tales*, A, 1077–9). Cf. *Anatomy*, III, ii, II, ii. (Shilleto, III, pp. 72 ff.)

Page 35

21. *Henry V*, II, ii, 135.

22. E.g. *Much Ado*, I, i, 60; *Romeo and Juliet*, I, iv, 47, II, iv, 80–1; *Twelfth Night*, IV, ii, 90; *Lear*, III, iv, 58. These references are often made by clowns or in jest. Aquinas (*Summa Theologica*, I, lxxviii, 4) gives the division of the five interior senses as in the text from Avicenna (*De Anima*, IV, 1), but denies the need to distinguish as Avicenna does between Fantasy, or the power of visualizing absent objects, and Imagination, or the power of dividing and combining imaginary forms. Aquinas therefore divides the inner powers of the soul into four: Common Sense, Imagination, and the estimative and memorative powers. Thomas Adams, in *The Mysticall Bedlam*, gives a different version of the five 'virtues' of the soul:

1. *Feeling*, whereby the Soul is moved to desire convenient things, and to eschew hurtfull. 2. *Witte*, whereby *she* knoweth sensible and present things. 3. *Imagination*, whereby *she* beholdeth the likeness of bodilie things, though absent. And these three virtues, say *Philosophers*, bee common to men with beasts. 4. is *Ratio*, whereby *she* judgeth between good and evill, truth and falsehood. 5. *Intellectus*, whereby *she* comprehends things (not onely visible but) intelligible, as God, Angels, &c. And these two last are peculiar to man, abiding with the *soule*, living in the flesh, and after death.

(*Works*, 1629, p. 493; cf. Batman, ff. 13 r⁰–14 v⁰.)

23. *Nosce Teipsum*, p. 46. The marginal note is 'The Imagination or Common Sense', which nicely illustrates the confusion that existed between the terms describing the different faculties of the mind.

24. Aristotle, *De Anima*, III, 1. Cf. Primaudaye, p. 366 ff.

Page 36

25. *Love's Labour's Lost*, I, i, 57 is the first reference given by the N.E.D. for the meaning 'native, untutored perception'.

26. *Anatomy*, I, i, II, vii. (Shilleto, I, p. 182.)

Page 37

27. Charron, *Of Wisdom*, tr. Lennard, pp. 67–8. Cf. Donne, *Elegie* XVII, ll. 50–5. (Grierson, I, pp. 114–5.)

28. *Merchant of Venice*, II, ix, 25–9. Cf. *Hamlet*, IV, iii, 4–5.
29. *Paradise Regained*, III, 47–56.
30. *Romeo and Juliet*, II, iii, 67–9. See below, pp. 141–4.

Page 38

31. *Merchant of Venice*, III, ii, 63–72. See C. R. Baskerville, *Bassanio as an Ideal Lover* (Manly Anniversary Papers (1923), pp. 90–103).
32. V, i, 41–7, 52–3 (ed. Parrott, p. 132). Cf. *Paradise Lost*, V, 100–13.
33. *Romeo and Juliet*, I, iv, 96–8. Nashe delivers an attack on the interpretation of dreams in *The Terrors of Night* (McKerrow, I, pp. 361 ff.) See below, p. 89.

Page 39

34. *Lingua* (by ? Thomas Tomkis), Act V, scene 18.
35. *John*, V, vii, 15–20.
36. *Richard II*, II, i, 31.
37. *Macbeth*, II, i, 38–9.

Page 40

38. *Midsummer Night's Dream*, V, i, 2–19. (In l. 14, 'airie' is the Q 1 reading, F 1 reads 'aire').

Page 41

39. *The Arte of English Poetry*, Bk. I, ch. viii. (*Elizabethan Critical Essays*, ed. Smith, Vol. II, pp. 19–20.)
40. *Hamlet*, III, iv, 71–2.
41. See Primaudaye, pp. 437–40.
42. Aristotle, *De Anima*, III, 10; cf. *Summa Theologica*, I, lxxx, 3. 'Appetite' is frequently used with the sense of 'unbridled passion' or 'sensual desire' (e.g. *Twelfth Night*, II, iv, 98–100; *Measure for Measure*, II, iv, 61; *Richard III*, III, v, 80; *Troilus and Cressida*, I, iii, 120, II, ii, 180–2; *Lear*, IV, vi, 125–6; *Othello*, III, iii, 269–71). The connection of thought between the Animal Appetite and the Voluntary Appetite may account for Shakespeare's association of Lust with Greed (see above, p. 19).

Page 42

43. Wright, p. 8.
44. *Summa Theologica*, I, lxxxi, 1–2.
45. Ibid., II, lxxiii, 1–4. Cf. Coeffeteau, pp. 32–6; Charron, pp. 73–4.
46. Coeffeteau, p. 9.

Page 43

47. Timothy Bright, in *A Treatise of Melancholy* (pp. 79–82) gives a

full classification of 'mixed passions'. He lists first the 'Simple Passions', which are either *Primitive*, as Love and Hate, or *Derivative*—i.e. Joy, Rejoicing, and Hope, which are derived from Love; and Heaviness, Sadness, and Fear, which are derived from Hate. Mixed Passions can be:
(i) *Compounds of Primitives*, either

   (a) Unequal mixtures of Love and Hate, i.e. Mirth (in which dislike of the event which has occurred is outweighed in our minds by gladness that it has not occurred to ourselves); and Pity (in which our dislike of the event out-weighs our liking for the person to whom it has happened).

   Or (b) Equal mixtures of Love and Hate, i.e. Envy and Jealousy.
Or (ii) *Compounds of Primitives and Derivatives*, i.e.:

   (a) compounds of Love—Trust (compounded of Love and and Hope), and Distrust (compounded of Love and Fear).

   (b) compounds of Hate—Anger (compounded of Hate and Hope for revenge), Bashfulness (compounded of Hate of oneself and Fear), and Malice (compounded of Hate of others and Anger).

Or (iii) *Compounds of Derivatives*—Despair (compounded of Grief and Fear), and Assurance (compounded of Joy and Hope).

48. Marston, *Antonio's Revenge*, I, ii, 275 (ed. Bullen, I, p. 119).

49. II, ii, 11–26 (Quarto 1601). (Works, ed. Herford and Simpson, III, p. 223.) Cf. *Lear*, IV, iii, 14–16.

Page 44

50. *Nosce Teipsum*, p. 48.

51. Primaudaye, p. 7; cf. Coeffeteau, pp. 56–7.

52. Primaudaye, loc. cit.

Page 45

53. *Faerie Queene*, II, i, lvii–viii; cf. Coeffeteau, p. 62.

54. For 'Will' =desire, see *Measure for Measure*, II, iv, 164; *Lear*, IV, vi, 278; *Lucrece*, l. 243; Sonnets CXXXV and CXXXVI.

55. *Nosce Teipsum*, p. 50.

56. Ibid., p. 52.

Page 46

57. Ibid., p. 49.

58. Davies of Hereford, *Microcosmos*, p. 230.

59. Primaudaye, pp. 424–5. Cf. *Hamlet*, I, ii, 50; *Troilus and Cressida*, II, ii, 116; *Twelfth Night*, IV, iii, 12.

60. *Nosce Teipsum*, p. 51.

Page 47

61. *Ecclesiastical Politie*, p. 14.
62. *Nosce Teipsum*, p. 52.
63. *Paradise Lost*, IX, 351–6.
64. Wright, p. 58. Cf. *Richard II*, II, ii, 14–27.

Page 48

65. Wright, p. 53.
66. Wright, pp. 53–4. Cf. *Hamlet*, III, iv, 85–8; *Winter's Tale*, IV, v, 481–4; *Troilus and Cressida*, II, ii, 58–60.
67. Coeffeteau, p. 55.
68. *Anthony and Cleopatra*, I, ii, 125–7, II, iii, 40.
69. p. 83.

Page 49

70. *Macbeth*, III, iv, 135–7; cf. *Richard III*, IV, ii, 63–5.
71. Wright, p. 54.

Page 50

72. Canto VI, st. 61–2. Theologically there was a distinction between *Conscience*, or the innate power of distinguishing Good from Evil, and *Synteresis*, the power which prescribed Good to the soul. There was a third power, *Syneidesis*, which passed judgement on acts already done. In common usage these finer distinctions were not maintained.
73. *Richard III*, V, iii, 180–2, 194–204. Cf. *Romeo and Juliet*, III, ii, 109–11; *Hamlet*, III, i, 50.
74. *Faerie Queene*, I, ix, xxxiii, ff.

Page 51

75. *Canterbury Tales*, I, 78–81. Cf. *Two Gentlemen of Verona*, V, iv, 79–81.
76. *Hamlet*, III, iii, 36–72.

Chapter Three

THE BODY

Page 53

1. This is the method used by Burton, (*Anatomy*, I, i, II, ii–iv; Shilleto, I, pp. 148–76.) Crooke (pp. 30 ff.) defends it as the best.
2. Cf. the quotations from Crooke, above p. 21.

3. *Anatomy*, I, ii, II, iv. (Shilleto, I, p. 176.) Cf. *Canterbury Tales*, A 1376, and edd. notes.

4. *Twelfth Night*, I, i, 36–7; cf. *Cymbeline*, V, v, 14, where the King calls Belarius, Guiderius and Arviragus 'the Liver, Heart and Braine of Britaine'.

Page 54

5. *Anatomy*, I, ii, II, iv. (Shilleto, I, p. 175.) Some (e.g. Ferrand, p. 71) tried to localize Love in the liver and Anger in the gall, but this was generally rejected (see Coeffeteau, pp. 21–2).

6. *Henry V*, V, ii, 166–70; cf. quotation from Crooke, above p. 21.

7. Concoction—the master-cook of the House of Alma (*Faerie Queene*, II, ix, xxx–i) was thought of as a gentle warming or boiling of the food.

8. Paré, *Works*, p. 12.

9. *Macbeth*, V, iii, 15; cf. 2 *Henry IV*, IV, iii, 104–5; *Twelfth Night*, III, ii, 62–5; *Merchant of Venice*, III, ii, 83–6.

10. Each concoction produced its own excrement. The first excrement, from the stomach, was thick—i.e. the faeces. The second, from the liver, was thin—i.e. urine. The third was either an invisible transpiration from the skin, or, according to Paré, was

'known sometimes by sweats, sometimes by a thicke fatty substance staining the shirt; sometimes by the generation of haire and nailes, whose matter is from the fulginous and earthy excrements of the Third Concoction.' (*Works*, p. 22.)

Hence Autolycus's 'Let me pocket up my Pedlers excrement' (*Winter's Tale*, IV, iii, 700–1). Cf. *Love's Labour's Lost*, V, i, 96–7; *Merchant of Venice*, III, ii, 87; *Hamlet*, III, iv, 121.

11. Lowe, *The Whole Course of Chirurgerie*, sig. D 2 v°.

Page 55

12. See Vicary, *The Anatomie of the Bodie of Man*, pp. 56–60, and cf. Crooke, pp. 370 ff., Primaudaye, p. 450. The belief that the Spirits were composed of a mixture of blood and air represents a (Galenic) combination of the Hippocratic theory of 'pneuma' with the belief that life resides in the blood.

13. *John*, V, vii, 52–6; *Lear*, V, iii, 217–8; *Othello*, III, iii, 262.

14. Fletcher, marginal note *h* on p. 19 of *The Purple Island*.

15. Crooke, p. 410; cf. Primaudaye, p. 564.

16. See Vicary, p. 32.

Page 56

17. *Anthony and Cleopatra*, IV, viii, 19–21. See Batman, f. 15 r°; and cf. Donne, *The Funerall*, ll. 9–11, and *The Progresse of the Soule*, ll. 501–5.

(Grierson, I, pp. 58, 315.) Behind these passages is the Galenic (ultimately Platonic) conception of Man as an 'inverted tree'—the brain being the root and the spinal cord and nerves the branches.

18. See below, pp. 88–9.

19. *Troilus and Cressida*, I, i, 60–1, III, iii, 105–6. Cf. *Hamlet*, III, iv, 119, and the quotation from Cornelius Agrippa above p. 34.

20. Batman, f. 17 v° seq. In Raphael's speech on the gradation of being (*Paradise Lost*, V, 469 ff.) mention is made of 'intellectual spirits' (l. 486). I do not know Milton's authority for this. The whole trend of the passage, however, is to emphasize the continuity of creation. This is likened to the springing of a plant from its roots (ll. 479–82), and the transition is made to the absorption of the plant as food and its metamorphosis into the spirits (ll. 482–5). These spirits give 'both life and sense, / Fansie and Understanding' and go on to become Reason (ll. 485–7). Now the highest faculties of the Soul—Reason and Understanding—are carried on without any corporeal activity, and should not need the offices of the Animal spirits, whose function it is to connect mental and bodily functions. Again, the intellectual functions of Angels differ from those of men. Angelic knowledge is purely intellectual; human knowledge is partly intellectual and partly sensitive—i.e. derived from the senses (*Summa Theologica*, I, liv, 3). Or as Milton says, Angelic knowledge is mainly intuitive, human knowledge mainly 'Discursive' or logical. Men do, however, possess some intuitive knowledge, and Milton seems to postulate a 'spirit' (perhaps with a sideglance at the use of 'spirit' to mean 'soul') which will make possible intuition and also the rational powers of the mind. This 'intellectual spirit' will then form a link between Men and Angels. It may also be regarded as the 'substance' of Angels, and in time men may come to discard the body and become, like Angels, pure intellect (ll. 493–503).

Page 57

21. Ll. 61–8 (Grierson, I, p. 53).

22. *Merchant of Venice*, V, i, 70–88. Cf. Bright, pp. 38–9, and above, pp. 24–6, 31.

23. *Tempest*, I, ii, 484–5.

Page 58

24. Batman, f. 29 r°. The ultimate sources of the Humoral theory were Hippocrates, *On the Nature of Man*, and Galen, *Of Temperaments* and *On the Natural Faculties*.

25. Lowe, sig. C 3 v°.

26. Batman, f. 29 v°. 'Working heat' =concoction.

27. Primaudaye, p. 523.

Page 59

28. Paré, p. 13.

29. Lemnius, *The Touchstone of Complexions*, tr. Newton, ff. 115 v⁰–118 v⁰.

30. Paré, p. 16.

31. *Touchstone*, ff. 132 v⁰ seq. We are not far here from Moth's 'seawater green complexion' (*Love's Labour's Lost*, I, ii, 79).

32. Langton, *An Introduction into Phisycke*, f. xlv r⁰ & v⁰.

Page 60

33. Ibid., f. xliv, r⁰ & v⁰. Others said that the sour melancholy had the function of sharpening the appetite and provoking excretion (see Batman, f. 33 v⁰.).

34. See Vicary, p. 71. 'Gall' is used some twenty times by Shakespeare as a noun, with the general sense of 'bitterness'. Twice (*Hamlet*, II, ii, 614–5; *Troilus and Cressida*, I, iii, 236) it has the sense of 'courage'. Shakespeare also uses 'gall' fourteen times as a verb, with the general sense of 'to irritate'.

35. See Crooke (pp. 181 ff.) for an account of the various theories of the function of the spleen. It was associated with laughter at least as early as Pliny the Elder (*Natural History*, Bk. XI, ch. lxxx). The phrase 'a merry spleen' in the sense of 'a whimsical frame of mind' was current in the early sixteenth century, and the senses 'sport, merriment, whim or caprice' were general by 1600. (N.E.D., s.v.) The sense 'bad temper, bitterness or irritability' which was also common at the end of the sixteenth century is probably connected with the fact that an obstruction of the spleen resulted in Jaundice. (According to Crooke, loc. cit., this would be black jaundice; yellow jaundice was produced by an excess of choler and resulted from an obstruction of the gall-bladder.) Cf. *Merchant of Venice*, I, i, 85–6 and *Troilus and Cressida*, I, iii, 2. A sense of 'spleen' peculiar to Shakespeare is that of 'speed' or 'haste', (*John*, II, i, 448, V, vii, 50; *Midsummer Night's Dream*, I, i, 145–6.) One would suppose that this sense arose from the use of the word in such phrases as 'acting in a spleen'—i.e. from a sudden whim or in a sudden fit of irritation.

36. The authorities often talk as if the ideal situation was an equal balance of the humours. Others say that the humours should occur in different amounts in the healthy body. Bright (pp. 4–5) says that Blood should have the majority; then in order Phlegm, Melancholy, and Choler.

Page 61

37. *The Opticke Glasse of Humours* (1607, London), f. 39 v⁰.; Bright, p. III.

Page 62

38. Aristotle, *De Generatione Animalium*, V, 741b, 8 ff.; 730b, 10–5. According to Langton, the liver was made from 'grosse blood', the heart from 'fine and subtle' blood mixed with spirits, and the brain from pure seed (f. xix r°, seq.). Cf. above, p. 53.

39. E.g. Lemnius, *Secret Miracles*, pp. 18 ff.

40. Crooke, p. 280.

41. Lemnius, *Secret Miracles*, pp. 11 ff. Cf. *Anatomy*, I, ii, III, ii. (Shilleto, I, p. 293.)

42. Huarte says that such children will only be exceptionally forward up to the age of 10, at which point the cold and dry temperature which they have inherited ceases to be an advantage and begins to hinder their development. (*Examination of Men's Wits*, tr. Carew, p. 315.) To be precocious was a bad sign in a child (cf. below, p. 67).

43. *Anatomy*, I, ii, I, vi. (Shilleto, I, pp. 244–5.)

Page 62

44. Huarte, pp. 282 ff., 320–1.

Page 64

45. Lemnius, *Secret Miracles*, p. 274.

46. Ibid., p. 310; cf. Crooke, pp. 272 ff.

Page 65

47. *Tamburlaine*, Pt. II, I, iv (ed Brooke, ll. 2590–603). It would be more logical if l. 2592 read 'Water and Earth', thus bringing together the two cold elements—air being hot and moist and therefore not unfavourable to virility. But doubtless Marlowe did not feel himself called on to maintain fidelity to strict theory. We may compare Henry IV's scornful characterization of Richard II (*1 Henry IV*, III, ii, 60 ff.) and Richard III's defiant account of himself (*Richard III*, I, i, 14 ff.).

Page 66

48. Wright, *A succinct Philosophicall declaration of the nature of Clymactericall yeeres*. For other divisions of Man's life, see T. F. Baldwin, *William Shakespeare's Small Latine and Less Greek*, Vol. I, pp. 657–73, and cf. *As You Like It*, II, viii, 137 ff.

49. *Works*, p. 9. Cf. Coeffeteau, pp. 655–71.

50. *Hamlet*, II, ii, 201–2.

51. *Timon*, II, ii, 218–23; cf. *Hamlet*, III, iv, 68–70. The coldness and thickness of the blood and the dullness and heaviness of the mind are symptoms of the 'earthy' humour of melancholy to which old men are prone. (See *Anatomy*, I, 2, I, v.)

L

52. Lemnius, *Touchstone*, f. 28 r°. Cf. *As You Like It*, II, iii, 46–53, and also *Paradise Lost*, XI, 527–43.

53. Whetstone, Dedication to *Promos and Cassandra* (1578). (*Elizabethan Critical Essays*, ed. Smith, I, p. 60.)

Page 67

54. Lemnius, *Secret Miracles*, p. 155. Cuffe explains that this is because such children have too little moisture in their constitution. Consequently their vital heat makes them soon ripe, but their bodies are quickly exhausted. (*The Differences of the Ages of Man's Life*, pp. 94–7.)

55. *Anatomy*, I, ii, II, i. (Shilleto, I, p. 247.)

56. See the table attached to f. 23 v° of John Jones: *The Bathes of Bathes Ayde*.

57. *Twelfth Night*, I, iii, 86–7.

Page 68

58. Huarte, pp. 289–90.

59. *Anatomy*, I, ii, II, i. (Shilleto, I, p. 250.) Cf. *2 Henry IV*, I, ii, 78.

60. Lowe, sig. E 2 v°, seq.

61. Langton, f. lxiiii, r°, seq.

62. Walkington, ff. 53 seq. For the same reason, tobacco was beneficial to phlegmatics and such as suffered from 'rheums' in the head.

Page 69

63. *The Taming of the Shrew*, Act IV, sc. i, iii.

64. Bright, pp. 250–7; *Anatomy*, I, ii, II, i. (Shilleto, I, pp. 247 ff.) Cf. also Du Laurens, *Discourse*, tr. Surphlet, pp. 104 ff.

65. Primaudaye, p. 820.

66. *2 Henry IV*, IV, iii, 95 ff.; cf. *Richard III*, V, iii, 73–5.

67. *Tamburlaine*, Pt. II, III, ii (ed. Brooke, ll. 3293–8).

68. *Macbeth*, I, vii, 64–8. Coeffeteau (p. 162) notes that choler is easily aroused in the drunk, as it is in Cassio.

Page 70

69. Lemnius, *Touchstone*, ff. 142 v°–143 r°.

70. Moorditch was the main drain for the Moorfields area. (See *1 Henry IV*, I, ii, 78–9 and edd. notes.)

71. *Anatomy*, I, ii, II, iii. (Shilleto, I, pp. 269–70.) Cf. the reference to the 'gib' (or castrated) cat in *1 Henry IV*, I, ii, 75.

Page 71

72. Paré, p. 12.

73. Cuffe, pp. 105–7.

74. *Coriolanus*, V, i, 47–58.
75. See Boorde, *The Regiment of Helth*, ch. iii.
76. *Julius Caesar*, II, i, 261–7.

Page 72
77. Lemnius, *Secret Miracles*, p. 191; cf. Crooke, p. 410.
78. Cf. *Troilus and Cressida*, V, i, 19–27; *Coriolanus*, I, iv, 30.
79. *Secret Miracles*, p. 192; cf. *Anatomy*, I, ii, II, vi. (Shilleto, I, p. 277).
80. Davies of Hereford, *Microcosmos*, pp. 66–7.
81. *Touchstone*, f. 17 v°.
82. Lowe, sig. C 2 r°. 'Melancholick' must here = 'choleric'; as has been noted, there was often confusion between these two humours. To Aaron may be compared Muly Mahomet in Peele's *The Battle of Alcazar*.

Page 73
83. *Microcosmos*, p. 63.
84. *Henry V*, III, v, 15–22. Cf. *Cymbeline*, V, ii, 3–4, V, v, 195–8.

Page 74
85. *Touchstone*, ff. 18 r°–19 r°.
86. Ibid., pp. 51 v°–52 r°.
87. *Anatomy*, I, ii, II, vi. (Shilleto, I, pp. 278–82.)
88. *Love's Labour's Lost*, IV, iii, 302–5.
89. Langton, f. lxxx v°.
90. Lemnius, *Touchstone*, pp. 56 v°–57 r°.

Page 75
91. *Macbeth*, II, ii, 38–9.
92. *Lear*, III, vi, 102–5 (omitted from Folio; text from Q 1608).
93. *Anatomy*, I, ii, I, i–iv. (Shilleto, I, pp. 202–39.)
94. Lemnius, *Secret Miracles*, p. 385.

Page 76
95. Lemnius, *Touchstone*, f. 23 v°.
96. *Hamlet*, II, ii, 639–42.
97. *The Discoverie of Witchcraft*, p. 52.

Page 77
98. See G. Zilboorg, *The Medical man and the Witch in the Renaissance*.
99. *Lear*, I, ii, 131–40.

Page 78
100. *Lear*, I, ii, 113–6.

101. Primaudaye, p. 711.

Page 79

102. Batman, ff. 129 v° seq.

Page 80

103. Fludd, *Microcosmi Historia*, Tome II, p. 63.
104. Batman, ff. 133 r° and v°. Vicary (p. 33) suggests that the brain itself moves in accord with the movements of the moon.
105. *Othello*, V, ii, 107–9.
106. *Twelfth Night*, I, iii, 140–2.

Page 81

107. Batman, ff. 126 seq.
108. The different planets had also special domination over the different ages of man's life. Thus, according to Cuffe (p. 121), Infancy is governed by the Moon; Boyhood by Mercury, which is 'inclining to *spitefulnesse, talke,* and *learning*'; Adolescence by Venus; Youth by the Sun; Manhood by Mars; Old Age by Jupiter; and Senility by Saturn. (Cf. *Microcosmos*, pp. 55–6.)

Apart from those quoted, Shakespeare's references to the stars are general. Throughout *Romeo and Juliet* there are hints of astrological influence, but these are never precise, in the way that Chaucer's are precise in *Troylus and Cryseyde*. Cassius and Hotspur, both choleric malcontents, resemble Edmund in their scepticism of celestial influence, (*Julius Caesar*, I, ii, 138–9; *1 Henry IV*, III, i, 13 ff.)

109. *Lear*, I, i, 294–5.

Chapter Four

THE BODY'S EFFECT ON THE SOUL

Page 82

1. Chapman, *Bussy D'Ambois*, III, i, 78–80 (ed. Parrott, p. 31).
2. *Lear*, II, iv, 106–10.

Page 83

3. Jones, *Galen's Bookes of Elements*, f. 3 v°.
4. Donne, *The Goodmorrowe*, l. 19 (Grierson, I, p. 8).
5. See Primaudaye, pp. 579–80.

6. Cf. Note 5 to Chapter II.

7. Primaudaye, p. 341.

8. *Anthony and Cleopatra*, V, ii, 288–9. Cf. Donne, *The Dissolution*, (Grierson, I, pp. 64–5).

9. *Pathomachia*, p. 2.

Page 84

10. *Henry V*, III, vii, 20–5.

11. Lemnius, *Touchstone*, f. 25 v°.

12. Ibid., Bk. I, ch. vi. Cf. Huarte, pp. 239 ff.; Walkington, ff. 77 seq; Langton, f. xvi r°, seq.

Page 85

13. IV, ii, 140–43. (*Shakespeare Apocrypha*, ed. Brooke, p. 338.)

14. *Julius Caesar*, V, v, 68–75. Cf. Donne, *Second Anniversarie*, ll. 122–46 (Grierson, I, pp. 254–5); Drayton, *Barrons Warres* (1603), p. 61.

15. *Cynthia's Revells*, II, iii, 123–30. (*Works*, ed. Herford and Simpson, IV, pp. 74–5.)

16. *Henry V*, II, ii, 127–40.

Page 86

17. For above, see Lemnius, *Touchstone*, Bk. I, ch. vii–x, and cf. Vicary, p. 41.

Page 87

18. Charron, p. 48; cf. Huarte, pp. 51 ff.

19. Primaudaye, pp. 417–8; cf. Wilson, *The Arte of Rhetoricke* (1553), f. 114 r° & v°. Cuffe (p. 125) notes that children have too moist and old men too dry brains to have good memories.

20. Charron, pp. 48–9. Barrough (f. 26 r°) notes that cold diseases, such as lethargy, cause loss of memory.

Page 88

21. *Hamlet*, III, iv, 142–4.

Page 89

22. Wright, p. 45.

23. Primaudaye, p. 526.

24. Walkington, f. 76 r°, seq.; cf. Du Laurens, pp. 95–6, Ferrand, pp. 178–85. This is perhaps more familiar to us in the shape of Dame Pertelote's advice to her husband (*Canterbury Tales*, B 4113 ff.).

Page 90

   25. *Hamlet*, II, ii, 614–6. Cf. Coeffeteau, p. 9:

      in like manner there are some creatures, which have desires,
      but no motions of choler; as for example, Sheepe, Pigeons and
      Turtles. . . .

   26. Coeffeteau, pp. 298–9; Primaudaye, pp. 455 ff.

   27. Bright, p. 91.

   28. Lemnius, *Secret Miracles*, p. 36.

Page 91

   29. Wright, p. 65. (I have altered the punctuation slightly to make
the meaning clearer.)

   30. Lemnius, *Secret Miracles*, p. 59.

Page 92

   31. *Hamlet*, I, iv, 23 ff. (Not in Folio; text from Q 2, ed. Parrott and
Craig, pp. 93–4.)

   32. For the characteristics of the four humours, see Lemnius, *Touchstone*, Bk. II, ch. ii, iii, v, vi; Walkington, ch. ix–xii; Paré, pp. 17–19;
Langton, f. xlii v°, seq.; Fludd, pp. 134–9; Du Laurens, pp. 84–5;
Batman, ff. 31 r° seq.; Primaudaye, pp. 534 ff.; *Regimen Sanitatis Salerni*,
tr. Paynell, ch. iii; etc. (Cf. also J. W. Draper, *The Humours and Shakespeare's Characters*. I cannot, however, agree with many of Professor
Draper's conclusions.)

Page 93

   33. IV, ii, 107–23 (ed. Brooke, p. 338).

   34. Bright, p. 96.

Page 94

   35. IV, ii, 85–98 (ed. Brooke, p. 338). These accounts are of course
ultimately based on those given of Lycurgus and Emetreus in *The
Knight's Tale* (*Canterbury Tales*, A 2128 ff.). Professor Curry (*Chaucer
and the medieval Sciences*, pp. 130 ff.) has shown reason for believing
that Lycurgus, who fights for Palamon, represents a Saturnian type,
and Emetreus, who fights for Arcite, a Martial type. *The Two Noble
Kinsmen* reverses their roles and, as I have suggested, seems to make
them rather representatives of the sanguine and choleric complexions.
Some of their original characteristics are retained, however, although
they are not strictly suitable: thus Palamon's champion has Emetreus'
curly hair, though this is not properly a trait of the sanguine, and
Arcite's champion has long straight hair like Lycurgus, though to him
curly hair would be more appropriate. There is no figure in *The*

Knight's Tale corresponding to the 'little freckled knight' of *The Two Noble Kinsmen*.

Page 95

36. *Anthony and Cleopatra*, III, iii, 11–20, 29–33.

Page 96

37. Bright, p. 98.
38. *John*, III, iii, 42–7. Cf. Batman, f. 33 rº.
39. Lemnius, *Touchstone*, f. 146 rº & vº. It is very tempting to speculate whether Shakespeare may have had memories of this passage when he wrote Act I, sc. v, of *Hamlet*. Hamlet, a melancholiac, swears by St. Patrick, having just seen a visitant from Purgatory who also speaks from underground, and being just about to swear his companions to silence. The combination of resemblances is at least striking.
40. *Anatomy*, I, i, III, i (Shilleto, I, p. 193.) Cf. Du Laurens, pp. 86–7.

Page 97

41. Bright, p. 99.
42. *Merchant of Venice*, I, i, 1–7.
43. Du Laurens, p. 84.

Page 98

44. Barrough, pp. 45–6.
45. See Lemnius, *Touchstone*, ff. 150 vº seq.; Du Laurens, pp. 100–4; Garzoni, pp. 16–18; Scott, pp. 53–4; Walkington, ff. 69 seq.; Lavater, *Of Ghosts and Spirits*, pp. 10–13; *Anatomy*, I, iii, I, iii. (Shilleto, I, pp. 462–5), II, ii, VI, ii. (Shilleto, II, pp. 131–2.)
46. *The Breviary of Helth*, f. lxxviii rº.
47. Dedication 'To the Right Worshipfull M. Peter Osbourne' (no pagination). Cf. ibid., pp. 187–93; *Anatomy*, III, iv, II, iv, v. (Shilleto, III, pp. 462–7.)
48. *Works*, p. 18. Cf. above, p. 89.

Page 99

49. Nashe, *The Terrors of Night* (*Works*, ed. McKerrow, I, p. 354).
50. Perkins, *A Discourse of the Damned Art of Witchcraft*, pp. 22 ff. Cf. Lavater, *Of Ghosts and Spirits* (ed. Wilson and Yardley), pp. 9–10.

Page 100

51. *The White Devil*, IV, i, 103–22. (*Works*, ed. Lucas, I, pp. 152–3.) Note that Francisco starts to speak to the ghost before he checks himself.

Page 101

52. *Discourse*, p. 82.
53. *Anatomy*, I, ii, III, iv. (Shilleto, I, p. 202.)
54. *Confessio Amantis*, III, 27–31. See N.E.D. under 'melancholy'.

Page 102

55. Bright, p. 108.
56. *Works*, p. 18.
57. Bright, pp. 109–11; *Anatomy*, I, i, III, iii. (Shilleto, I, pp. 197–9.)
58. Lemnius, *Touchstone*, f. 147 r⁰.
59. Langton, f. xlvi r⁰. But see below, p. 105.
60. Primaudaye, p. 535.
61. *Bussy D'Ambois*, III, ii, 450–8 (ed. Parrott, p. 44).

Page 103

62. Du Laurens, pp. 88–9. Cf. *Anatomy*, I, i, III, iv. (Shilleto, I, pp. 199–202.)
63. See above, pp. 100–1.
64. Garzoni, p. 19; cf. *Duchess of Malfy*, Act V, sc. ii.
65. Cf. *Canterbury Tales*, A 1373–4 and edd. notes, and Professor Lowes' article on 'Heroic Melancholy' (Mod. Phil., XI, pp. 491 ff.). Ferrand (pp. 25–6) attributes Love melancholy to 'windy' or hypochondriacal melancholy because the Liver is traditionally the seat of Love.
66. See N.E.D., under 'Humour'. There are two peaks in Shakespeare's use of the term. The first occurs in plays written about 1593–5: *Richard III, Comedy of Errors, Taming of the Shrew, Romeo and Juliet*, and *King John*. The second, which may be connected with Jonson's and Chapman's popularization of the term, occurs in plays written about 1598–1600: *1* and *2 Henry IV, Henry V, Merry Wives, Much Ado*, and *Julius Caesar*. It is most frequent in *The Merry Wives*, where it is used twenty-one times. In the *Dramatis Personae* of *The Merry Wives* (Q 1602) Falstaff and his companions are called 'irregular humorists', (Cf. *Hamlet*, II, ii, 339–40.) After this second peak Shakespeare's use of the word is infrequent.
67. Samuel Rowlands, *The Letting of Humours Blood in the Head Veine*, Epigram 27, ll. 1–2. Cf. Nym, in *The Merry Wives*, and Sogliardo, in *Every Man out of his Humour*, of whom Mitis says: 'why, this fellowes discourse were nothing, but for the word Humour.' (II, i, 56–7, ed. cit., III, p. 461.)

Page 104

68. Ll. 98–109 (ed. cit., III, pp. 431–2).

69. Prologue, ll. 5–9 (ed. cit., V, p. 294).

70. *Letting of Humours Blood*, Introduction *To the Gentlemen Readers*, ll. 1–2, 7–8, 35–6 (sig. A 2 r° & v°).

Page 105

71. Aristotle, *Problems*, Bk. xxx, I. (Loeb edition, pp. 155 ff.) I am much indebted in what follows to L. Babb, *The Background to Il Penseroso* (Stud. Phil., XXXVII (1940), pp. 257–73). The same author's *The Elizabethan Malady* was not published until after this chapter was written.

72. Charron, p. 49.

73. Bright, p. 126.

74. Du Laurens, p. 86.

75. Cf. quotation from Du Laurens, below p. 106.

76. *Touchstone*, f. 147 r°.

Page 106

77. Walkington, f. 64 v°. Walkington is, however, hostile to the idea that melancholiacs may be of good intellect. He says they may be ingenious in villainy but never 'good wits', and it is foolish to desire this complexion (f. 67 r°.).

78. Loeb ed., p. 161.

Page 107

79. Du Laurens, p. 85.

80. Ll. 9–14. (*Works*, ed. Bullen, III, p. 307.)

81. Persius, Satire I, ll. 11–12: 'nolo: / quid faciam? sed sum petulanti splene: cachinno.' Cf. quotation from *The Scourge of Villainie* above and see O. J. Campbell, *Comicall Satyre and Shakespeare's Troilus and Cressida*, esp. ch. II.

Page 108

82. Lemnius, *Touchstone*, f. 136 v°. (Incorrectly paginated in original.)

83. V, ii, 99–104. (*Works*, ed. Bond, III, p. 155.) Cf. *Thomas Lord Cromwell*, III, ii, 101–5. (*Shakespeare Apocrypha*, p. 177.)

84. *Love's Labour's Lost*, I, i, 227–9; cf. I, ii, 1–2.

85. II, iii, 68 ff. (ed. cit., III, p. 228). Both Puntarvolo in *Every Man out of his Humour* (II, ii) and Daw in *The Silent Woman* (II, ii) affect melancholy.

86. Among epigrammatists, see Hall, *Virgidemiarum* (1598), p. 37; Cooke, *Epigrams served out in fifty-two several dishes*, No. 8; Marston, Satires appended to *Pygmalion's Image*, II, ll. 127 ff.; Rich, *Opinion Defied*, p. 53. Among character-writers, see Hall, *Characters*, p. 99–105;

Overbury, *Works,* ed. Rimbault, pp. 73-4; Rich, *My Ladies Looking Glass,* p. 53; Earle, *Microcosmographie,* no. 6; Saltonstall, *Picturae Loquentes* no. 8.

87. See the description of Hyselophronus in Davies of Hereford, *Humours Heaven on Earth,* st. 12–15.

88. Cf. Harington, *The Metamorphosis of AIAX,* sig. A 8 r⁰; *Hamlet,* II, i, 77 ff.

89. See the frontispiece to Rowlands, *The Melancholick Knight,* and cf. *Love's Labour's Lost,* III, i, 13–4, *Macbeth,* IV, ii, 208, and Jonson, *The Devil is an Ass,* I, i, 51.

90. *Love's Labour's Lost,* III, i, 15–17; *Two Gentlemen,* II, i, 16–18; *Titus Andronicus,* III, ii, 4. Cf. the portrait of 'Inamorato' in the frontispiece to *The Anatomy of Melancholy* (3rd Edition, 1628).

91. *The Knight of the Burning Pestle,* II, viii, 14–15. Cf. below, p. 138.

Page 109

92. *Merchant of Venice,* I, i, 101–2.

93. *Works,* ed. McKerrow, I, pp. 169–70. Cf. Rich, *Faults, Faults, and nothing else but Faults,* p. 7.

94. *The Repentance of Robert Greene* (*Works,* ed. Grosart, XII, p. 172). Cf. Nashe, *The Unfortunate Traveller* (*Works,* ed. McKerrow, II, pp. 300–2), and see Z. S. Fink, *Jaques and the Malcontent Traveller* (Phil. Quart., XIV (1935), pp. 237–55).

95. Satires appended to *Pygmalion's Image,* II, ll. 139–56. (*Works,* ed. Bullen, III, pp. 274–5.)

Page 110

96. *Skialethia,* Satyre V (sig. D 6 r⁰.).

97. *The Philosophers Satyres,* pp. 9–10. Cf. Donne's Fourth Satire (Grierson, I, pp. 158–68) the subject of which has elements of the malcontent, the traveller, the politician, the intelligencer, and a hint of the Jesuit as well.

Page 111

98. III, ii, 47 (*Works,* ed. Bullen, I, p. 51).

99. *Every Man out of his Humour:* 'The Character of the Persons' (ed. cit., III, p. 423).

100. See O. J. Campbell, *Jaques* (Huntingdon Library Bulletin No. 8 (Oct. 1935), pp. 71–102. The cause of Jaques' melancholy is never made clear in *As You Like It.*

Page 112

101. *The Malcontent,* I, i, 243, 26–37, 201–9.

102. See E. E. Stoll, *Shakespeare, Marston and the Malcontent Type* (Mod. Phil., III (1906), pp. 1 ff.) and O. J. Campbell, *Shakespeare's Satire*, pp. 142 ff.

103. He had also, in Aaron, drawn a melancholic villain (cf. *Titus Andronicus*, II, iii, 30–6).

Page 113

104. *Problems* (Loeb ed.), p. 169.

105. Walkington, f. 67 v°.

106. Burton excepts fools from the catalogue of those who may become sufferers from melancholy. (*Anatomy*, I, i, III, ii; Shilleto, I, p. 196.) Madmen have hot brains, and are consequently instable of purpose, while melancholiacs are of a cold temperature. Lemnius, however, (*Touchstone*, f. 18 v°) says that those who have their minds inordinately fixed upon revenge find it difficult to settle on any resolution.

107. *Tamburlaine*, Pt. II, IV, i. (ed. Brooke, ll. 3700–5).

Page 114

108. *The White Devil*, III, ii, 314 ff. (*Works*, ed. Lucas, I, p. 145).

109. *The Duchess of Malfy*, I, i, 24–9, 79–84; III, iii, 50–7.

110. Ibid., V, ii, 180.

111. Ibid., II, i, 74–84.

Page 115

112. Vindice, in *The Revenger's Tragedy* adopts in pursuit of his revenge the pose of the blunt, satirical, 'familiar rogue', and as such dilates on the evil lusts of the world (Act I, sc. iii). He has, however, no other contact with Hamlet except his brooding over the skull of his dead mistress, with which he enters at the beginning of the play. Ford's *The Lover's Melancholy* (1628) has some interest in that it is heavily indebted to Burton. See especially III, iii, where a masque of melancholiacs is presented before the love-sick Prince Palador.

113. *Timon*, IV, iii, 201–3; cf. 238–41.

114. Ibid., IV, iii, 298–9.

Chapter Five

THE SOUL'S EFFECT ON THE BODY

Page 119

1. *The Copie of a letter written by E. D., Doctour of Physicke*, pp. 14–5.

Page 120

2. I, iv, 205–20 (ed. cit., III, p. 219). Cf. Sonnet CXLVII.

3. Wright, p. 60.
4. Paré, p. 39.

Page 121

5. I, ii, 244–8. (*Works*, ed. Bullen, I, p. 118.) Cf. *Merchant of Venice*, III, ii, 111–4.
6. Wright, pp. 61–2.
7. *Macbeth*, V, iii, 40–6.
8. III, i, 8–19. (*Comedies*, ed. Parrott, pp. 334–5.)
9. Coeffeteau, p. 333.

Page 122

10. *Edward I*, sc. xxix, ll. 200 ff. (*Works*, ed. Bullen, I, p. 212.)
11. Primaudaye, p. 471.
12. *Macbeth*, V, iii, 11–12, 14–17. Cf. *John*, IV, ii, 106–7; *Richard III*, III, v, 1–4.
13. Paré, p. 40. Cf. *Hamlet*, III, iv, 120–2; *Macbeth*, V, v, 11–13.
14. Primaudaye, p. 471.

Page 123

15. Ibid., p. 497.
16. Coeffeteau, p. 602.
17. *Richard II*, II, i, 115–9.
18. E.g., *3 Henry VI*, II, i, 79–84.
19. *Richard II*, III, iii, 140–1; *Coriolanus*, V, vi, 102–3. Cf. *3 Henry VI*, II, ii, 111; *Richard III*, IV, i, 33–5.

Page 124

20. *Lear*, II, iv, 56–8 (cf. II, iv, 122); *Winter's Tale*, I, ii, 110–1. Cf. *Titus Andronicus*, III, ii, 7–11.
21. Jorden, f. 5 r° & v°. Cf. Drayton, *Polyolbion*, Song VI, ll. 19–28.
22. Primaudaye, p. 510.
23. Bright, p. 93. Shakespeare uses 'stomach' in the sense of 'Pride' (e.g., *Henry VIII*, IV, ii, 33–5); 'Courage' (e.g., *Henry V*, IV, iii, 35; *Troilus and Cressida*, II, ii, 134–5); and 'Anger' or 'Resentment' (e.g., *Lear*, V, iii, 94–5; *Titus Andronicus*, III, i, 232–3).
24. Primaudaye, p. 510.
25. Paré, p. 39.

Page 125

26. *Tamburlaine*, Pt. II, IV, i (ed. Brooke, ll. 3852–5).
27. Ibid., V, iii (ll. 4476–7, 4485–9).
28. Coeffeteau, pp. 604–5.

29. Primaudaye, p. 506.

30. Ferrand, p. 7.

31. See Du Laurens, pp. 117 ff. and cf. above, p. 103 and n. 65 to Ch. IV. Chaucer describes himself as suffering from melancholy as a result of love at the beginning of *The Book of the Duchess*, ll. 1–40.

Page 126

32. Coeffeteau, p. 169. With what follows, cf. L. Babb, *The Physiological Concept of Love in Elizabethan and early Stuart Drama* (P.M.L.A., LVI (1941), pp. 1020 ff.

33. *Measure for Measure*, II, iv, 19–26.

34. Coeffeteau, p. 169. Cf. *Hamlet*, III, iv, 72–6.

Page 127

35. *Troilus and Cressida*, III, ii, 17–24.

36. *Faerie Queene*, III, x, lix.

37. Paré, p. 40.

Page 128

38. *Lear*, V, iii, 197–200.

39. Bright, p. 154.

40. See *2 Henry IV*, III, ii, 59–64; *Much Ado*, III, i, 77–8; *Midsummer Night's Dream*, III, ii, 97; *Merchant of Venice*, I, i, 82; *Hamlet*, IV, vii, 123. This notion, which is also frequent in Elizabethan literature outside Shakespeare, may result from the fact that Grief and Sorrow dry up the blood; consequently the signs of grief may by extension be said to exhaust it.

41. Bright, pp. 134–43.

42. Ibid., pp. 146–7.

Page 129

43. Ibid., pp. 157–8.

44. *Duchess of Malfy*, III, iii, 65–7 (ed. Lucas, II, p. 82).

45. Essay *Of Friendship*. (*Works*, ed. cit., VI, pp. 437–8.)

46. *Macbeth*, IV, iii, 209–11; cf. *Titus Andronicus*, II, iv, 34–7; *Much Ado*, III, i, 78.

47. *Hamlet*, I, ii, 158–9; cf. *Richard II*, II, i, 228–9.

Page 130

48. Wright, p. 27. With what follows, cf. Craig, *Shakespeare's Depiction of Passion* (Phil. Quart. XIV (1935), pp. 189 ff.); Walker, *Convention in Shakespeare's Description of Emotion* (Phil. Quart., XVII (1938), pp. 28 ff.).

49. Paré, p. 40.

50. *The Second Anniversarie*, ll. 244–6. (Grierson, I, p. 258.)
51. *Microcosmos*, p. 91.
52. E.g. *Richard II*, I, iii, 208–9. In *Love's Labour's Lost* the function of the eye is compared to that of Rhetoric, the art of displaying and stimulating emotion. (*Love's Labour's Lost*, II, i, 228–30, III, iii, 27–8; cf. II, i, 234–48, V, ii, 827.)
53. *Troilus and Cressida*, III, ii, 36–9; cf. Wright, p. 29.
54. For what follows, see Wright, pp. 131–2; 'Arcandam', sig. N 5 r° seq.; Hill, *The Contemplation of Mankind*, ff. 14 r° seq., 218 r°, 220 v°.

Page 131

55. *Faerie Queene*, III, i, xli.
56. *3 Henry VI*, I, iv, 116–8.
57. Cf. *Paradise Lost*, IV, 114–23.

Page 132

58. *Othello*, I, i, 61–5; *Richard III*, III, i, 7–11.
59. *Macbeth*, I, v, 62–3, III, ii, 27–8, V, v, 10–13.
60. *Winter's Tale*, I, ii, 368–75; cf. *Henry VIII*, I, i, 125–9, III, ii, 205–8.

Page 133

61. *John*, IV, ii, 69–70. Cf. *2 Henry IV*, I, i, 60, ff.
62. Cf. B. L. Joseph, *Elizabethan Acting*, ch. III, esp. pp. 49, 54–5.
63. *Hamlet*, II, ii, 587–93. (In l. 590. F reads 'warmed'.)

Page 134

64. Donne, *The Goodmorrowe*, l. 16 (Grierson, I, p. 7.)
65. Wright, p. 42.
66. III, i, 60–8. (*Works*, ed. Bullen, II, p. 162.)
67. *Julius Caesar*, I, ii, 190–3. Ferrand (p. 167) may give us a further hint of Cassius' appearance on the stage: 'those that have little, dry, hollow eyes, with a long, thin, wrinkled visage, are lewd, crafty, slaunderous, envious, covetous, treacherous, sacrilegious rascally fellowes: *Especially, if they are wont to looke very stedfastly on any thing, and use to bite their lips when they are thinking of their business.* . . .'(my italics).

Page 135

68. Ferrand, p. 172. Langton (f. xvii v°) says that the most temperate part of the body is 'the skynne of the myddeste of the paulme of the hand'. If this was hot, therefore, the rest of the body must be even more distempered. Lemnius (*Secret Miracles*, pp. 109–10) says that an artery runs down to the fourth or ring finger, and consequently many

wear rings of gold upon that finger, so that the beneficial influence of the gold may be conveyed to the heart. We still wear our gold wedding-rings upon the fourth finger of the left hand. (Gold approached most nearly of any terrestial substance to the perfect mixture of the elements, and was consequently free from rust and decay. It was because of this that it was used as a medicine, especially in the form of *aurum potabile*.)

69. *Othello*, III, iv, 36–44; cf. *Anthony and Cleopatra*, I, ii, 46–50.
70. 'Arcandam', sig. B 3 v°.

Page 136

71. Lemnius, *Secret Miracles*, p. 38.
72. Hill, ff. 12 seq.; cf. 'Arcandam', sig. M 5 v° seq.
73. Hill, ff. 15 seq.
74. Ferrand, p. 143.

Page 137

75. Coeffeteau, pp. 427–8.
76. Hill, ff. 205 v°–206 r°.
77. Hill, ff. 206 v°–207 r°.
78. *Hamlet*, III, ii, 266–7; cf. *Richard III*, III, v, 5–11.
79. 'Arcandam', sig. P 8 r°.

Page 138

80. Hill, f. 205 r°.
81. Hill, f. 206 v°.
82. *I Henry IV*, III, ii, 60.
83. *Touchstone*, f. 36 v°.
84. 'Arcandam', sig. P 4 r° & v°.
85. Hill, f. 133 v°.

Page 139

86. Hill, f. 133 r° & v°.
87. Ferrand, p. 169.
88. *Macbeth*, I, iv, 11–14; cf. *Duchess of Malfy*, I, i, 249–53.
89. *Secret Miracles*, p. 131.
90. *Richard III*, I, i, I. ff.
91. *Hymne to Beautie*, ll. 113–9; cf. *John*, III, i, 43–54.

Page 140

92. Charron, pp. 18, 20.
93. Romei, p. 23.
94. Huarte, p. 281. Cf. Bacon, *Of Beauty* (ed. cit., VI, pp. 478–80).
95. Vaughan, *Directions for Health* (1626), p. 131. Cf. *Merchant of Venice* l, iii, 99–101.

Page 141

96. Ferrand, pp. 223–5.

97. *Paradise Lost*, VIII, 530–3; cf. *Tamburlaine*, Pt. I, V, ii (ed. Brooke, ll. 1941–63).

98. Coeffeteau, pp. 85 ff.

99. Ferrand, p. 32. Cf. *Anatomy*, III, ii, III, i. (Shilleto, III, pp. 178–80.)

100. *Troilus and Cressida*, V, ii, 103–8. Cf. above, pp. 37–8.

Page 142

101. *Anatomy*, III, i, I, ii. (Shilleto, III, pp. 15 ff.) Coeffeteau (p. 97) distinguishes five kinds of Love by adding the Love of Angels and the Love of God.

102. *Anatomy*, III, i, III. (Shilleto, III, pp. 32 ff.)

103. *Anatomy*, III, ii, I, ii. (Shilleto, III, pp. 55–7.) Burton leaves this passage in the decency of Latin.

104. Book IV of the *Faerie Queene* is entirely devoted to this virtue. See especially Canto ix, st. i and ii, which Burton quotes with approval (Shilleto, III, p. 34).

105. See L. E. Pearson, *Elizabethan Love Conventions*, pp. 252 ff.

Page 143

106. Donne, *A Valediction of the Booke*, ll. 35–6. (Grierson, I, p. 31.)

107. Spenser, *Epithalamium*, l. 86. Cf. also Lovel's disquisition on the nature of Ideal Love in Jonson's *The New Inn*, III, ii. (ed. cit,. VI, pp. 453 ff.).

108. Charron, p. 43.

109. *Much Ado*, IV, i, 97–105.

Page 144

110. Charron, p. 20.

111. *Othello*, V, ii, 6.

Chapter Six

CONCLUSION

Page 147

1. *2 Henry IV*, V, v, 47. For parallels between the King and the heart, see Forset, pp. 29 ff.

2. See L. C. T. Forrest, in *P.M.L.A.*, LXI (1946), pp. 651 ff.; A. L.

Walker, in *Phil. Quart.*, XVII (1938), pp. 28 ff.; E. E. Stoll, in *M.L.N.*, LIV (1939), pp. 79 ff.

3. Paracelsus and his followers, for example, held a radically different view of the nature of Man and his soul.

Page 149

4. In *Hamlet* the evil is outside the hero; his tragedy is that as the instrument of retribution he must himself sin and be punished; *Julius Caesar* is a political play, and would be better classed with the histories. (Cf. L. B. Campbell, *Shakespeare's Tragic Heroes*, esp. ch. I and II.)

M

BIBLIOGRAPHY

ADAMS, THOMAS, *Works*, 1629.

AGRIPPA, HEINRICH CORNELIUS, *Three Books of Occult Philosophy*. Tr. J. Freak, 1651. (1st Latin edition, 1531.)

ALLEN, D. C., 'The Degeneration of Man and Renaissance Pessimism.' (*Stud. Phil.* XXXII (1938), 202 ff.)

ANDERSON, M. L., 'Elizabethan Psychology and Shakespeare's Plays.' (*Univ. of Iowa Humanistic Studies*, 1927.)

ANON, *Pathomachia, or the Battle of the Affections*, 1630.

ANTHONY, ROBERT, *The Philosophers Satyres*, 1616.

ARCANDAM (pseud.), *The Most excellent Profitable and pleasant book, of the famous Doctor and expert Astrologian Arcandam or Alcandren. . . . Now newly turned out of the French into our Vulgar tongue*, by William Warde, 1592.

BABB, L., 'The Background of *Il Penseroso*' (*Stud. Phil.*, XXXVII (1940) 257 ff.).

'The Physiological Concept of Love in Elizabethan and early Stuart Drama' (*P.M.L.A.*, LVI (1941), 1020 ff.).

BACON, FRANCIS, *Works*, ed. Spedding, Ellis and Head, London, 1858.

BALDWIN, T. F., *William Shakespeare's Small Latin and Less Greek* (Urbana, 1947).

BARCKLEY, SIR RICHARD, *A Discourse of the Felicitie of Man*, 1598.

BARROUGH, PHILIP, *The Method of Phisicke*, 3rd Edition, 1596. (1st Edition, 1583.)

BASKERVILLE, C. R., 'Bassanio as an Ideal Lover' (*Manly Anniversary Papers* (1923), 90 ff.).

BATEMAN, STEPHEN, Bartholomeus Anglicanus, *De Proprietatibus Rerum* ('Batman on Bartolome'), 1582.

BEAUMONT, FRANCIS, and FLETCHER, JOHN, *Selected Plays*, ed. J. St. L. Strachey (Mermaid Edition), 1904.

BOORDE, ANDREW, *The Breviary of Helth*, 1557.

The Regiment or Dietary of Helth, 1562.

BRIGHT, TIMOTHY, *A Treatise of Melancholy*, 1586.

BURTON, ROBERT, *The Anatomy of Melancholy*, ed. A. R. Shilleto, London, 1893.

CAMPBELL, L. B., *Shakespeare's Tragic Heroes* (C.U.P., 1930).

CAMPBELL, O. J., 'Jaques' (Huntingdon Library Bulletin, No. 8 (Oct.,

1935), 71 ff.). 'Comicall Satyre and Shakespeare's *Troilus and Cressida* (Huntingdon Library Publications, 1938).

Shakespeare's Satire (O.U.P., 1943).

CASTIGLIONE, BALDASSARE, *The Book of the Courtier*, tr. Sir Thomas Hoby, 1561 (ed.W. B. D. Henderson (Everyman Library), 1928).

CHAPMAN, GEORGE, *Tragedies*, ed. T. M. Parrott, London, 1910.

Comedies, ed. T. M. Parrott, London, 1914.

CHARRON, PIERRE, *Of Wisdom*, 3 books, tr. Samson Lennard, 1607.

CHAUCER, GEOFFREY, *Works*, ed. W. W. Skeat, Oxford, 1894.

COEFFETEAU, NICHOLAS, *The Table of Humane Passions*, tr. Edward Grimestone, 1621.

COOKE, JOHN (?), *Epigrams served out in 52 several Dishes*, by I. C., n. d. (*c.* 1604).

CRAIG, H., *The Enchanted Glass* (N.Y., 1936).

'Shakespeare's Depiction of Passion' (*Phil. Quart.*, XIV (1935), 189 ff.).

CROOKE, HELKIAH, *Microcosmographia. A Description of the body of Man*, 1618.

CUFFE, HENRY, *The Differences of the Ages of Man's Life*, 1607.

CURRY, W. C., *Chaucer and the Mediaeval Sciences* (N.Y., 1926).

D., E., *The Copie of a letter written by E. D. Doctour of Physicke to a gentleman by whom it was publisht*, 1606.

DAVIES, SIR JOHN, *Orchestra*, 1596.

Nosce Teipsum, 1599.

DAVIES, JOHN (of Hereford), *Humours Heaven on Earth*, 1601.

Microcosmos: The Discovery of the Little World, with the Government thereof, 1603.

DONNE, JOHN, *Poetical Works*, ed. H. J. C. Grierson, Oxford, 1912.

DOWDEN, E., *Essays Modern and Elizabethan* (London, 1910).

DRAPER, J. W., *The Humours and Shakespeare's Characters*. (Durham, N.C. 1945.)

DRAYTON, MICHAEL, *The Barrons Warres*, 1603.

Polyolbion, 1622.

EARLE, JOHN, *Microcosmographie*, 1628

ELYOT, SIR THOMAS, *The Book named the Governor*, 1531 (ed. F. Watson (Everyman Library), 1907).

FERRAND, JACQUES, *Erotomania, or A Treatise Discoursing of the Essence, Causes, Symptomes, Prognostics, and Cure of Love or Erotique Melancholy*. Tr. Edmund Chilmead, 1640. (1st French Edition, 1612.)

FINK, Z. S., 'Jaques and the Malcontent Traveller' (*Phil Quart.*, XIV (1935), 237 ff.).

FLETCHER, JOHN, *see* BEAUMONT, FRANCIS

FLETCHER, PHINEAS, *The Purple Island*, 1633.

FLUDD, ROBERT, *Microcosmi Historia*, 1619.

FORD, JOHN, *Selected Plays*, ed. Havelock Ellis (Mermaid Edition), 1888.

FORREST, L. T. C., 'A Caveat for Critics against invoking Elizabethan Psychology' (*P.M.L.A.*, LXI (1946), 651 ff.).

FORSET, EDWARD, *A Comparative Discourse of the Bodies natural and politique*, 1606.

GARZONI, TOMASO, *The Hospital of Incurable Fooles*, tr. Anon, 1600.

GOWER, JOHN, *Works*, ed. G. C. Macauley, Oxford, 1899.

GREENE, ROBERT, *Works*, ed. R. B. Grosart, London, 1881–6.

GUILPIN, EVERARD, *Skialetheia, or A Shadow of Truth*, 1598.

HALL, JOSEPH, *Virgidemiarum, the Three last Books*, 1598.
Characters of Vertues and Vices, 1608.
Works, 1625.

HARINGTON, SIR JOHN, *The Metamorphosis of AJAX*, 1596.

HEYWOOD, THOMAS, *A Woman Kill'd with Kindness*, 1607 ('Third Edition.').

HILL, THOMAS, *The Contemplation of Mankinde*, 1571.

HOOKER, RICHARD, *The Laws of Ecclesiasticall Politie*, 1611.

HUARTE, JUAN, *The Examination of Mens Wits*, tr. R(ichard) C(arew), 1594.

JONES, JOHN, *The Bathes of Bathes Ayde*, 1572.
Galens Bookes of Elementes, 1574.

JONSON, BEN, *Works*, ed. C. H. Herford and P. Simpson, Oxford, 1925—.

JORDEN, EDWARD, *A Briefe Discourse of a Disease called the Suffocation of the Mother*, 1603.

JOSEPH, B. L., *Elizabethan Acting* (O.U.P., 1951).

KYD, THOMAS, *Works*, ed. F. S. Boas, Oxford, 1901.

LANGTON, CHRISTOPHER, *An Introduction into Phisycke*, 1562.

LAURENS, ANDRE DU, *A Discourse of the Preservation of the Sight; of Melancholike Diseases; of Rheumes and of Old Age*. Tr. Richard Surphlet, 1599. (Shakespeare Association Facsimiles, No. 15, 1938.)

LAVATER, LEWES, *Of Ghosts and Spirites walking by Night*, tr. R(ichard) H(aydock), 1572. (ed. J. D. Wilson and M. Yardley, Oxford, 1929.)

LEMNIUS, LEVINUS (Ludvig Lemmens), *The Touchstone of Complexions*, tr. Thomas Newton, 1576.
The Secret Miracles of Nature, tr. Anon. 1658. (1st Latin edition, 1571.)

LOVEJOY, A. O., *The Great Chain of Being* (Cambridge, Mass., 1936).

LOWE, PETER, *The Whole Course of Chirurgerie*, 1597.

LOWES, J. L., 'The loveris maladye of Hereos' (*M.P.*, XI (1913), 491 ff.).

LYLY, JOHN, *Works*, ed. R. W. Bond, Oxford, 1902.

MARLOWE, CHRISTOPHER, *Works*, ed. C. F. Tucker Brooke, Oxford, 1910.

MARSTON, JOHN, *Works*, ed., A. H. Bullen, London, 1887.

MILTON, JOHN, *Poetical Works*, ed. H. C. Beeching, Oxford, 1904.

NASHE, THOMAS, *Works*, ed. R. B. McKerrow, Oxford, 1904–10.

OVERBURY, SIR THOMAS, *Works* ed. E. F. Rimbault, London, 1856.

PARE, AMBROISE, *The Works of that famous Chirurgeon Ambrose Parey*, tr. by Thomas Johnson, 1634.

PAYNELL, THOMAS (tr.), *Regimen Sanitatis Salerni*, 1530.

PEARSON, L. E., *Elizabethan Love Conventions* (Berkeley, Cal., 1931).

PEELE, GEORGE, *Works*, ed. A. H. Bullen, London, 1888.

PERKINS, WILLIAM, *A Discourse of the Damned Arte of Witchcraft*, 1608.

POPE, ALEXANDER, *Essay on Man*, 1732–4. (ed. M. Mack (Twickenham edition) 1950.)

PRIMAUDAYE, PIERRE DE LA, *The French Academie*, tr. Thomas Bowes, *et al.*, 1618. (1st French editions, 1577–90; partly translated into English, 1584, 1594, 1601.)

RICH, BARNABE, *Faults, Faults, and nothing else but Faults*, 1606.

My Ladies Looking-Glasse, 1616.

ROMEI, ANNIBALE, *The Courtier's Academy*, tr. J. K(eper), n.d. (1598).

ROWLANDS, SAMUEL, *The Letting of Humours Blood in the Headvein*, 1600.

The Melancholick Knight, 1615.

SALTONSTALL, WYE, *Picturae Loquentes*, 1631.

SCOT, REGINALD, *The Discovery of Witchcraft*, 1584.

SHAKESPEARE, WILLIAM, *Sonnets*, 1609.

Works, 1623.

Plays, ed. W. J. Craig, *et al.* (Arden edition), London, 1899–1924.

The Shakespeare Apocrypha, ed. C. F. Tucker Brooke, Oxford, 1908.

The Second Quarto Hamlet, ed. T. M. Parrott and H. Craig, Princeton, 1938.

King Lear, 1608 (Shakespeare Quarto Facsimiles, No. 1, 1929).

SMITH, G. G. (ed.), *Elizabethan Critical Essays*, Oxford, 1904.

SPENCER, T., *Shakespeare and the Nature of Man* (C.U.P., 1943).

SPENSER, EDMUND, *The Faerie Queene*, ed. J. C. Smith, Oxford, 1909.

Minor Poems, ed. E. de Selincourt, Oxford, 1910.

The Variorum Spenser, ed. E. Greenlaw, *et al.*, (Johns Hopkins, 1933.)

STOLL, E. E., 'Shakespeare, Marston and the Malcontent Type' (*Mod. Phil.*, III (1906), 1 ff.).

'Jaques and the Antiquaries' (*M.L.N.*, LIV (1939), 79 ff.).

THORNDIKE, L., *A History of Magic and Experimental Science* (N.Y., 1923–34.).

TILLYARD, E. M. W., *The Elizabethan World Picture* (London, 1943).

TOMKIS, THOMAS, *Lingua, or the Combat of the Tongue and the Five Senses for Supremacy*, 1607.

VAUGHAN, WILLIAM, *Directions for Health*, Sixth Edition, 1626. (1st Edition, 1600.)

VICARY, THOMAS, *The Anatomie of the Bodie of Man*, 1548 (ed. F. J. and P. Furnivall (E.E.T.S.) 1888).

WALKER, A. L., 'Convention in Shakespeare's Description of Emotion (*Phil. Quart.*, XVII (1938), 28 ff.).

WALKINGTON, THOMAS, *The Opticke Glasse of Humours*, London 1607.

WEBSTER, JOHN, *Works*, ed. F. L. Lucas, London, 1927.

WILSON, SIR THOMAS, *The Arte of Rhetoricke*, 1553.

WRIGHT, THOMAS, *The Passions of the Mind in Generall*, 1604.

A Succinct Philosophicall Account of the nature of Climactericall Yeeres, occasioned by the Death of Queen Elizabeth, 1604.

ZILBOORG, G., *The Medical Man and the Witch in the Renaissance* (Johns Hopkins, 1935).

INDEX

I. OF SUBJECTS

II. OF AUTHORS QUOTED OR REFERRED TO